$15.95

Particularly Peculiar People

Barbara Gibson Taylor

For my family

...some of whom are still speaking to me

...and especially for Zanne who was there when the man said, "What the hell d'ya pick the damn flar fer?"

I hold dear in my heart the following people who gently nudged B. Lynn through the birth canal and then had the fortitude to stick around and help raise her to maturity:

Rick Ohler, my teacher and friend, and the members of Rick's Thursday afternoon memoir class and Tuesday night creative writing class. Thank you for keeping B. Lynn alive beyond the age of twelve. If not for you, I would have gladly killed her. Kind and gracious people, all.

Over countless way-too-early-in-the-morning breakfasts in local diners, we told each other: we can do it. Consuming unreasonable portions of Stouffer's macaroni and cheese during a blizzard, we told each other: we can do it. Gazing across platters of burned bacon, we told each other: we can do it. My dear friend: you did it. Thank you, Kateri Ewing, for showing me the way.

Thank you, Bob Herrmann, for your patience and willingness to peruse, letter-by-letter and word-by-word, *Particularly Peculiar People*. You have my endless gratitude.

Randy, Zanne, Courtney and Jamie: you read and read and read my stories, and always asked for more; there is no better form of encouragement. Thank you for your suggestions, most of your opinions, your constant support and for always being there. I love you.

Introduction

My mother always said engaging in unpleasant activities builds character. She most often said this to my sister and me. I don't recall her ever saying it to herself. As a result, my sister and I developed masochistic tendencies, ever vigilant that our characters weren't having too much fun.

Sprawled on the couch one winter day, enjoying the sloth and gluttony that occurs on a winter day, of many winter days in Western New York, my mother's words wriggled into my carbohydrate stunned brain: my character was finding life far too pleasurable. Grunting off the couch, I shuffled around the house looking for a distasteful business that would make me feel better about myself.

Lying on the kitchen table was a brochure that arrives in the mail twice a year. They have never received my consideration because they announce themselves as Adult Education. I have never been interested in learning how to behave like an adult and I don't understand people who are.

Scanning the one-and-a-half pages of information I was surprised to discover that not only did it offer lessons in maturity, but several others with which to make myself miserable. My eyes snagged on Writing Memoir and Family History. I reflected on this for a moment and decided it might be just the thing: pawing through the sludge in my brain to write a memoir was sure to provoke anxiety and depression, because most of my life has not been interesting and I would just as soon forget the parts that were. I figured attending a few sessions would probably get my character straightened-up at least until spring, when I could do something else that felt like self-abuse; I signed up for the course because I hated the very thought of it.

I went to the first class and it was an uncomfortable two hours so I knew it was improving my character. As I was pulling into the driveway after the third class, my stomach started screaming at my mouth to prepare for an imminent delivery: I dashed into my house just in time to spew verbiage all over the kitchen floor.

Over the next several weeks I threw-up so many nouns, adjectives and verbs that word debris sifted through the house like feathers in a chicken coop after Mr. Fox has come a 'calling. I'd no sooner get one mess cleaned up when I'd start gagging on conjunctions and flakes of punctuation.

Sweeping up after a particularly violent episode of heaving, I noticed there were some pretty good words in my dustpan. I dumped them onto my desk and spent the next several days pushing them around into various arrangements.

Then I vomited B. Lynn. She gushed out of my mouth and splatted onto my desk like a rotted pumpkin. At first I didn't recognize her, so coated was she in memory muck. But when I grabbed her up and rinsed her off in the kitchen sink, the cleaner she became the more she looked familiar. When I saw I was holding my alter-ego, B. Lynn, I was so startled I dropped her in the sink. I hadn't realized I still had her in me. Over the years I listened to plenty of stories about my B. Lynn-self so my first inclination was to stuff her down the garbage disposal.

I remembered how my father's hands would tremble when he whispered about how, as a toddler, she stumbled around the house with a wet washcloth draped over her head, plucking up bit and pieces of floor junk—the stray fingernail clipping and such. She tucked her findings under her chin and continued wandering in search of more treasure—knocking into the furniture and upsetting the dog, what with the washcloth hanging in her eyes.

Blowing violent plumes of cigarette smoke, my mother would hiss that when she tried to hold B. Lynn as a baby she thrashed and screamed, yanked her hair and clawed at her face like a schizophrenic spider monkey. Terrified of the child, my mother would dump her in her crib until she howled the demons out of herself.

Their landlord, living below them in the first floor apartment, harbored a great dislike of priests. Believing B. Lynn was eventually going to require an exorcism, and loathe to let a priest cross his threshold, he gave my parents a week's notice to pack up their belongings and get out of his house— *and don't forget to take the kid.* My mother would sigh and say it was the nicest apartment they ever had.

My sister, Zanne, already traumatized at the tender age of six years by the unfortunate arrival of a sibling, refused to talk about her.

I watched B. Lynn squall and writhe in the kitchen sink; having knowledge of her disagreeable reputation made me reluctant to handle her. After a few minutes of uneasy observation, I quickly snatched her up by one rubbery little leg, crammed her on the top shelf of a basement closet and slammed the door. I should have known that wouldn't contain her.

At times, when I was sitting at my desk scrupulously recording the things I did on my summer vacations, I would feel my hackles rise. Before I could figure out what my hackles were—and what was causing them to rise, B. Lynn would clamp her sticky fingers over my eyes—*Guess who?* I'd reach over my shoulder and fling her to the floor but then she'd latch onto my leg and stay stuck on my shin like a pricky little cocklebur.

One evening, as I was moodily arranging words that were refusing to resolve themselves into sentences, B. Lynn crawled under my desk and began sucking on my big toe. I looked down and studied her; she looked up and studied me. Sighing, I hauled her onto my lap and brushed the hair out of her eyes. She squinted at the computer screen and said, "Pretty boring stuff, this." I agreed, but reminded her that this pastime was good for our characters.

B. Lynn slammed her hands down on the keyboard and said, "To heck with your life—let's tell about mine. I can write it without character—I can write it without conscience, too." So I gave my word collection to B. Lynn and let her write her own stories.

My sister says her tales are nothing but lies. Of course they are. B. Lynn always was a very good liar.

Contents

Playing with Boys

The house at 124 Prescott Street is trembling on its foundation. It shakes and shudders. A startled shingle jumps off the roof and hides in the hollyhocks, a hairline fracture in the living room window blossoms into a spider web of defeated glass.

The racket coming from within the house reverberates through the neighborhood. Housewives pause in their dusting to cross themselves and thank the good Lord that the five-year-old child manufacturing the disturbance doesn't belong to them. They mutter about what they would do to the child's rear end as they listen to her shriek and howl like a rabid puppy confronted with its water bowl.

The bawling and pounding of floors at 124 Prescott Street continue until B. Lynn's mother is of the same opinion as the neighbors about what needs to be done to the child's rear end, and there is *finally some PEACE and QUIET, for crying out loud.* B. Lynn finds herself in her bedroom with a stinging rear-end and plenty of time to fume about her first morning of kindergarten, with a teacher who doesn't know the first thing about anything.

B. Lynn loves boys. She loves the games they play: tackle football, cowboys and Indians, cops and robbers; she loves the clothes they wear: t-shirts and belted dungarees that give her the freedom to climb trees and roll in the grass without displaying her underpants. She is a marvelous fighter and she excels at spitting. Because she is so very good at behaving like a boy—in fact, she is a better boy than most boys—she believes she is one.

This misconception has occurred through no fault of her parents, who have attempted on numerous occasions to make their younger daughter understand that she suffers from gender confusion. But—because they have told her a number of things that are not true—B. Lynn has little faith in their credibility. She believes she's a girl as much as she believes there isn't a wolf living under her bed or her toy vacuum cleaner won't come to life in the middle of the night and suck her out of her blankets. Her parents eventually succumb to B. Lynn fatigue and realize life is more pleasant at 124 Prescott Street when they let their daughter believe she is, what she is not.

For a brief period of time, the boys on Prescott Street make the regrettable error of referring to B. Lynn as a girl. She corrects their foolish notions by bloodying their noses, pummeling their stomachs, and bending their fingers backward until the hapless boys fall to their knees: *Awright—AWRIGHT! You're a boy, let go—let GO for cripessakes—you're a BOY! JEEZ!* After observing her teaching methods the girls in the neighborhood don't voice their opinions on the subject.

Because no one has volunteered to display the irrefutable evidence that B. Lynn is not a boy—indeed, she isn't even aware any evidence exists—and because she has everyone in her small world properly trained about her identity, she spends her first five years happily believing she holds a respectable position in the male kingdom... until the first day of school with a teacher—a woman with only a KINDERGARTEN education—who insists that B. Lynn is a girl. For the next several years she will encounter the same problem with all her teachers, despite their higher levels of learning.

When B. Lynn reaches twelve years of age, her biological clock shrieks on high noon. Her adolescent hormones reconfigure her mind and her body and she discovers she actually loves being a girl—playing with boys.

Gone to the Dogs

She looked as if a mean-spirited dog assembler had hastily slapped her together with leftover bits and pieces of canine parts. Her long ears suggested a hint of cocker spaniel; her muzzle that of a German shepherd. The assembler pinned the long legs of an Irish setter onto her hind end and then maliciously stuck the short legs of a beagle onto her front end. This arrangement of her legs caused her to be slanted.

For unknown reasons, a large portion of her tail had been amputated at birth. She wasn't much given to wagging it, anyway. A wad of blonde hair grew beneath the unhappy stump; it issued from her rear end like an old cushion spilling its stuffing. B. Lynn's mother referred to this nether hirsuteness as her underpants. Because of the unfortunate location of the hair it was often clumpy and matted and B. Lynn's mother would yell, *Don't touch her underpants, for crying out loud.*

As a puppy, she left small bodies of water all over the house and so was given the apt, if not original, name Puddles. When she was behaving decently she was affectionately called by variables of her name: Pud, Puddy, Puddy-Pup. She didn't respond to any of them and she didn't return the affection. Perhaps the early hacking on her tail gave her cause to distrust the overtures of humans.

B. Lynn's optimistic attempts to cuddle the cur were quickly rebuffed. Puddles struggled out of her sticky embraces and with the heavy sigh of a long-suffering martyr, flopped herself down in another location. Undeterred, B. Lynn crawled after her. The dog and child repeated their sequence: hug—move—flop—crawl, and continued this marvelous game until her mother took pity on the sorry animal and tied her up in the backyard. (The dog.)

Raised together from infancy, Puddles and B. Lynn were inseparable. They were a single entity. When B. Lynn went missing, her mother was likely to ask, *Where's PUD?* She didn't bother calling for B. Lynn because she didn't respond to her name any better than the dog. Puddles was a well-known presence in the neighborhood. Lacking any notion of loyalty to her family, she wandered from house to house looking for handouts and took up residence wherever she found good food. As B. Lynn grew older, it was her job to hunt for the dog and drag her home. It was B. Lynn's older sister's job to hunt for Puddles and B. Lynn and drag them both home.

When the summer sun warmed the asphalt, Puddles slumbered peacefully in the middle of the street luxuriating in the heated tar, clumps of gravel clinging to her fur like warts on a fat toad. The neighbors, familiar with her indifference to commands, carefully negotiated their cars around her. Strangers to Prescott Street slammed on their brakes. When they realized she wasn't dead, they beat on their horns and called her names that didn't even come close to being a variation of Puddles. Keeping an eye on her dog from her front porch, B. Lynn would shout, "Drive around her—drive AROUND her. Jeesh."

The dog answered to no one. She was obstinate. She was incorrigible. She was B. Lynn's best friend.

***

Years later, B. Lynn languishes in a Psychology 101 class. The drone of the professor's voice as he reads from the textbook is lulling her to sleep. His words roll around in her head, exit through her ears, and then drip onto her desk—until he says something that lodges in her neglected cerebrum. She abruptly sits up and flips through her book to find the section being droned. Narrowing her eyes, she scans the page: *The duckling learns to follow...* "Uh-huh" *...can occur with any object, not necessarily the mother...* "Yep" *... forms a lifelong association...* "Okay" *... establishes an individual preference for a certain species...*

B. Lynn slaps her hand on her desk, slumps in her chair and says, "Good GOD. I imprinted with a MONGREL."

A People Person

B. Lynn sits motionless and staring at the mess of earthworms wriggling on her plate. She is so involved with the display that when her mother enters the breakfast room and clears her throat, she convulsively flings her fork across the room and back-pedals her chair away from the table. She glances up at her mother and then back to her plate, where the worms have arranged themselves into complacent noodles.

B. Lynn sits motionless and staring at her mother. It is a toss-up as to whether she is more terrified of the worms on her plate or the woman standing in front of her. She listens carefully to what her mother is telling her, but her brain fumbles with the word-seeds she is scattering around in her head: *playing i with Prescott want any more street you the don't kids. our they're of people kind not.*

B. Lynn sits motionless and staring at the mural on the breakfast room wall. It is an idyllic scene of mountains and forest but if she looks at it long enough, she will see wolves slink out from behind the trees. While her eyes are busy looking for wolves, the words suddenly line up into another ridiculous sentence that doesn't make plain sense: *I don't want you playing with the Prescott Street kids any more. They're not our kind of people.*

***

B. Lynn sits motionless and staring, surveying her universe from her front porch and chewing the word-seeds her mother planted in her head. She is fairly certain she's the same kind of people as everyone else in the neighborhood but she can't figure what kind of people her mother is.

Mary Catherine scuffs down the sidewalk on her scooter. When B. Lynn is in the mood to be a girl, Mary Catherine is her best friend. They pray together in their bedroom closets, asking God to make their parents let them spend the night together.

When B. Lynn was permanently suspended from the First Presbyterian Sunday School for pitching a violent tantrum on her first morning of attendance, Mary Catherine assumed the role of teacher for her religious education. She has even taught her the proper Roman Catholic prayer procedure. B. Lynn suspects that even God won't be able to save her if her mother catches her crossing herself in the closet.

Mary Catherine's mother speaks with an Italian accent and eats dinner with her elbow on the table, head propped on her hand. Mary Catherine has been taught that eating meat on Fridays is a sin. B. Lynn has been taught that eating with your elbows on the table is a sin that will send you to hell as quickly as saying *shut up.*

B. Lynn's eyes slide past Mary Catherine and settle on Marvin. Marvin is in love with B. Lynn, and on rainy mornings he is charged with the task of clearing the sidewalks of worms so she can walk to school without hyperventilating or fainting.

Marvin lives with his parents and a couple of grandparents who are kept sequestered in a small room off the kitchen. His grandmother has a goiter the size of a basketball. It thrusts her head so far back that she is forced to spend her life looking up at heaven. She is so old, B. Lynn is surprised she isn't already there.

Marvin kneels in the grass on one knee, pretending to tie his shoe—but everyone knows what he is really doing—what he is really doing is taking a moment to defile his pants even though he is seven-years-old.

Anthony skips down the sidewalk, stands in front of Marvin with his hands on his hips and screams, *Marvin Poopy-Pants.* He runs away before Marvin finishes his business.

Anthony's mother is dead. His father doesn't want him so he lives with his nonnie. He happily offers this piece of information as if he's bragging about catching the biggest fish. But after his father has made a rare visit and leaves him behind when he returns to Syracuse with his new wife and children, Anthony cries and runs into his house to bring a picture of his mother outside. *See? This is my mother! She's beautiful, isn't she? Isn't she beautiful? She's DEAD.*

The telephone rings in B. Lynn's kitchen and she hears her teenage sister, Soozie-Bells, pound across the upstairs hallway like a rhino in heat. She hangs over the stairway bannister breathless for a phone call from anyone. Their mother answers the phone. It is Georgie's mother. She is calling because she is worried that one of these days B. Lynn is going to get hurt playing tackle football with the older boys. Her mother tells her, *You should be more worried about the boys.*

Georgie is B. Lynn's best boyfriend. When the other kids aren't around they sneak into his father's toolshed behind the garage and play a game of their own creation: Secretary. Taking turns, they exchange roles as boss and secretary. The secretary sits on the boss's lap and receives a chaste kiss on the cheek. It is titillating.

Georgie's father is a swaggering, squatty, bulldog of a man with a brush cut and fists like boiled hams. A former sergeant in the Marine Corps, he enjoys reliving his days as a man of consequence so he periodically engages in hand-to-hand combat with Georgie's mother.

Georgie stands outside in the DMZ with all the other excited kids in the neighborhood, and listens to his mother scream when his father's hams splat on her face. Sometimes the furniture gets involved in the melee. Georgie giggles, dances from foot-to-foot and clutches the front of his pants, as he waits for his turn to play war with his father.

Hilda Leibowitz hunches down the sidewalk, her string bag sagging from her arm. She is on her daily journey to the grocery store and it is the only time she makes herself available for public viewing. Her gray hair, pulled back in a severe bun, and her wire-rimmed glasses make B. Lynn think of the gramma wolf in Little Red Riding Hood. B. Lynn would be less afraid of the wolf. Hilda leads a cloistered life in a dull house of faded paint and sagging doors, her only companion a lone goose that resides in her garage.

Little Toot, Smelly Belly, Baby Kid and a cat named Fats live next door to Hilda, their houses separated by a thin ghost of a gravel driveway. Little Toot, Smelly Belly, Baby Kid and the cat named Fats, own the only mother who allows all the neighborhood kids to play in her house—even when it isn't raining. Plus she lets them drink Kool-Aid out of brightly colored aluminum glasses.

Although they are a family with peculiar names, and Smelly Belly throws temper tantrums until she passes out cold on the ground, this is the family most like B. Lynn's because her mother says they are wasps. B. Lynn has never witnessed any buzzing aggression from them—but she has been told where her own stinger is located—it's in her mouth.

B. Lynn squints at the house on the corner. She is alternately terrified and fascinated with the place. Her mother told her it's the oldest house on the block and it used to be a barn when the end of Prescott Street was a swamp.

There are gravestones in the foundation of the basement— B. Lynn has SEEN them. The house is a huge box of a place that wears listless brown asbestos shingles. Patsy lives there in the second-floor flat with her parents, an aunt and an uncle. B.

25

Lynn finds Patsy particularly annoying, so she is glad she has to live in a house that has gravestones in the basement.

Patsy's mother, father, aunt and uncle, are permanent fixtures on the front porch. They creak slowing to and fro in their rocking chairs and entertain themselves with watching and yelling at Patsy all day.

They are currently creaking, watching and yelling, from a muddy hole because the porch floor eventually collapsed from rocker abuse. But the hole suits Patsy's family just fine, and they will continue to sit in it until they have saved enough money to build a concrete porch.

John's parents are quite often on the porch, or in the porch hole, rocking with Patsy's family. John lives, in noisy disarray, in the first-floor flat with his parents, three brothers, and two dogs. They have a tangled familial relationship with Patsy's parents. John's mother is a large raw-boned woman with a booming barking manner of speech and she makes B. Lynn crave baked goods: *Looks like it's gonna rain—don' it? This hamburger smells off—don' it? My living room looks good all rearranged—don' it?* She also refers to the bathroom as "the John," and B. Lynn can't figure why she would name her youngest son after a toilet.

B. Lynn believes John is the ideal All American Boy: he is a scientist, chef, a working man and a juvenile delinquent. Although he is several years older than B. Lynn—almost a teenager—and despite his proclivity for crime, he is gentle with her and allows her to follow him around like an infatuated puppy.

In a cramped bedroom he shares with one of his brothers, John performs delicate surgery on a variety of small creatures. Slicing open their bellies, he solemnly examines the tiny hearts, livers and lungs. When he has finished poking around in the red gelatinous mush, he pops out the eyeballs with his small scalpel, puts them in little jars of formaldehyde, and gives them to B. Lynn. She places them on her science shelf in her bedroom with the other miracles of nature he has given her: a bird's nest holding a shattered blue egg, a papery fish bladder, a stone that might be an arrowhead; locust husks and a vial of liquid mercury that has magical properties.

An accomplished chef, John prepares fried bologna on his Sterno stove. B. Lynn squats in the grass beside him and watches as he carefully melts butter in his rusty iron frying pan. He shows her how to cut into the edges of the bologna before cooking so it doesn't curl. Sautéing the bologna until it is just short of black, he then serves it between slices of floppy Wonder Bread. His fried bologna sandwiches are the best things she will ever eat in her life.

A blue wooden Buffalo Evening News box hunkers between the curb and the sidewalk in front of his house; John is the only kid in the neighborhood with a real job. He teaches B. Lynn how to fold and tuck the newspapers into sturdy missiles, and on the occasional Sunday morning, he lets her sit on the crossbar of his bicycle and fling the newspapers in the general direction of his customers' houses.

Old Zeke pumps past on his derelict bicycle. He rides down Prescott Street several times a day. B. Lynn doesn't know where he comes from, where he is going, or if his real name is Zeke, but when he makes an appearance it is a Prescott Street custom to scream: *Hey Zeke!* She leans over the porch railing and screams, *Hey Zeke!* He never responds to the greetings because he is always engaged in earnest conversations with himself.

The front screen door whines open and B. Lynn's mother shoves their dog, Puddy-Pup, out onto the porch. The door bangs shut with the sharp report of a gunshot and Puddy-Pup, dull and stupid with sleeping, looks around baffled to suddenly find herself outside when only moments before she had been enjoying a forbidden nap on the sofa.

B. Lynn snaps her fingers and makes kissing noises. "C'mere, girl—smooch- smooch. C'mon, good doggie—smooch-smooch. Puddy-Pup, COME HERE." Puddy-Pup yawns, stares glumly at B. Lynn and then plods down the porch steps. She ambles along the front sidewalk and into the street.

Sniffing the pavement, Puddy-Pup staggers around in a circle a few times before collapsing onto the warm asphalt. B. Lynn stands up and claps her hands. "PUDDY! COME!" Because B. Lynn is inconsequential to her well-being, Puddy-Pup ignores her. She flops back into her chair and wishes she had a dog like Lassie.

A big old Plymouth rolls slowly down the street and B. Lynn waits to see if the driver will steer around her dog or stop and beat on the car horn like a fool. It is Mrs. Hill from down the street and she is well aware of Puddy-Pup's ambivalence about being run over. Her car crunches in the gravel shoulder and slides past Puddy-Pup who is impersonating a dead dog, asleep on her back with all fours legs stuck straight up in the air.

B. Lynn lifts her hand to wave but Mrs. Hill keeps her eyes, hiding behind sun glasses, straight forward. B. Lynn can't figure why she's wearing sunglasses when the neighborhood is so shady, but then she remembers that Mrs. Hill stayed up late playing tag with her husband. Maybe her eyes are tired.

The night before, peering out from under her bedroom window shade, she watched Mr. Hill chase Mrs. Hill—wearing her nightgown, for crying out loud—down the street. They raced through tree shadows cast by streetlights, Mrs. Hill shrieking like a scalded cat. B. Lynn can't wait to be a grown-up so she can play outside at two o'clock in the morning.

A silent police car arrived, the dome flicking red in the trees and briefly high-lighting Mrs. Hill's left eye, swelled-up to the size of a purple Easter egg. The policeman made Mrs. Hill forfeit the game of tag to her husband. The policeman told her to go home and stop making a racket because decent people were trying to get some sleep.

Mrs. Hill looked dispirited about losing the game to her husband but she took his outstretched hand, mewling like a kitten that knows it's going to be bundled in a burlap bag and tossed into the river. B. Lynn can't decide which would be worse: having a policeman make you lose a game or forgetting to put on all of your clothes before going outside to play.

B. Lynn thinks about finding Georgie to see if he wants to work on the forts they're building in the field that's called the woods. Georgie and B. Lynn are the bosses of the field that's called the woods and they need to get down there to finish the forts while the other kids aren't around to mess everything up. They need to get everything ready so when the other kids are around she and Georgie can tell them all the rules.

She stands up and then quickly slumps back into her chair when she sees Ramona sneaking into the field that's called the woods. Ramona is generally disliked; she is unlikeable. She lies and cheats and gets kids into trouble for things that don't count because the kids had only made MISTAKES.

Although her personality defects are not uncommon in the neighborhood, in Ramona they are unacceptable: she is considered a foreigner because she lives around the block. As such, she is she not allowed the same privileges as real Prescott Street kids.

B. Lynn is currently engaged in hostilities with Ramona because she told her mother about B. Lynn's scientific experiment with fire. She told her mother that B. Lynn almost

burned up the field the way the trees—that were the woods—
burned up a long time ago.

Ramona is not only a squealer, she is a scolder. Planting
her hands on her hips, she leans forward from her waist and
then wags her finger in her victim's face. Ramona's squealing
and scolding, combined with her big red face and straight
yellow bangs, make B. Lynn think she might be related to
Porky Pig.

The milk truck pulls over to the curb down the street and B.
Lynn's mouth waters for a chunk of the ice that chills the
bottles of milk. She thinks briefly of running over to ask for a
piece, but old Nina beats her to it. Nina doesn't want a piece of
ice, but she would like a piece of the milkman. Nina loves the
milkman. She loves the bakery man. She loves the mailman,
the Sweet Kleen man, the boy who delivers Charles Chips and
the meter reader. B. Lynn snorts when the milkman starts
acting silly and laughing way too loud. He walks back to his
truck with his chest puffed out like a rooster on his way to
cockfight.

Nina is a woman of an unfortunate age who does not
realize she lost her fortunate age years ago. Stuffed into a pair
of—*Who wears short*—shorts and a red tube-like top that
reveals a freckled overflowing bosom and a python-esque roll
of flesh wrapped around her waist, Nina minces around her
yard in high heels and large straw hats as she tends her flowers.

She dyes her hair in varying shades of red and B. Lynn's
mother says she wears six inches of make-up. B. Lynn would
like to know what she's hiding under the half-foot of
Maybelline's Sun Kissed Bronze, and the tangerine lipstick
that strays beyond the boundaries of her lips. She wonders if
she wears big hats in the hot sun so her face won't melt and
slide right off her head.

Nina is a conundrum: although suitably married, she isn't a mother, she doesn't act like a mother, but one of the Pagano boys says she's a mighty fine looking mother. Lacking children, she slathers her disappointed maternal instincts on a small, beige, gooey-eyed, unworthy representative of the canine species. The nasty creature wears a pink bow on its head and is malignantly unapproachable. Its name is Susie. Nina also keeps stacks of cages behind her garage that house soft furry bunnies that she cuddles and strokes. Then she sells them as food to people who have a taste for the flesh of soft furry bunnies.

Nina's presence is a source of aggravation to all the neighborhood kids. Her yard is one of the few on the block that is strictly off limits for trampling and general destruction. She also stands out like a brilliant tropical bird in a neighborhood of faded gray pigeons, thus igniting their predatory instincts.

When the neighborhood kids get tired of fighting with each other, they gather on the sidewalk across the street from her house and chant, *That'll be the day when Nina goes away!* B. Lynn uneasily participates in these hostilities, but she isn't convinced that Nina needs to go anywhere. She doesn't tell the other kids that Nina sets aside special treats for her on Halloween, or that she has been invited into her house and allowed to hold her prized Jerry Mahoney ventriloquist doll.

B. Lynn sits motionless and staring at the leaf faces peering out from the lilac bush in her front yard. She is still pretty sure that everyone in the neighborhood is her kind of people—but she is stunned senseless with a sudden thought: do the people in the neighborhood think she is THEIR kind of people? She chokes on the word seed she has been chewing.

And so, for the rest of her life, whenever she meets someone new, B. Lynn will wonder: *Are you my kind of people?* Or—of greater concern—*Am I YOUR kind of people?*

Trespasser

B. Lynn's mother would like her daughter to look like Shirley Temple. Her daughter, B. Lynn, would like to look like the Lone Ranger. Her mother thinks if her daughter's hair looks as pleasant as Shirley Temple's, her brain might soak up the idea and make the rest of her body behave in a cute way. B. Lynn thinks if she looks like the Lone Ranger she might get a horse—and if she got a horse she'd gallop all the way to Hollywood and yank every hair out of Shirley Temple's obnoxious head.

Because B. Lynn's hair resembles a jumble of brown Pick-Up Sticks, her mother has to resort to artificial means in order to achieve the desired Shirley Temple effect. Unsnagging the last of the bobby pins that have clawed her scalp all night like anteaters rummaging for termites, her mother gives her hair an optimistic fluff and tells her to get dressed for church.

Her mother is walking her Sunday walk, which is unlike her weekday walk. Her Sunday walk is stiff with the righteousness of someone who is preparing for church—or someone who has just returned from church. Her weekday walk is that of a supple feline prowling for a morsel of mouse. Both walks make B. Lynn uneasy and she wishes her mother would take up crawling—a much less aggressive way of getting around.

After sitting quietly for a moment, B. Lynn slinks down the hallway to the bathroom. She stretches over the yawning mouth of the sink and grabs hold of the faucet nose with both hands, kicking and belly squirming until she has hauled herself up onto the sink's lower lip. Balancing on her shins, she stares into the mirror: her head looks as though it is spawning Slinkys.

She twists the sink's white-gloved fingers and slides back down to the floor. When the faucet nose is running warm, she thrusts her head under the water until her hair is running wet. She pads softly back to her bedroom and contemplates her church shoes.

Twenty minutes later B. Lynn is standing on the sidewalk in front of her house, waiting for her family to finish fashioning themselves into decent looking Presbyterians. She picks at the front of her dress where the smocking is nibbling her chest like fire ants feasting on a carcass. Reaching under her dress she tugs at her Sunday underpants that are generally troublesome.

Her mother stalks out the front door and stops so suddenly she sways like a TV antenna in high wind, and it occurs to B. Lynn it would be a wonderful thing if she could take off her bare feet and hide them behind her back. Her mother drags her pitchfork eyes from B. Lynn's seaweed hair down to her bare feet, rasps them back up from her feet to her hair.

Deciding to save the subject of dripping hair for something fun to discuss during the long Sunday afternoon, her mother flatly asks, *Where are your shoes.*

Because her mother is perfectly aware rapid blinking is a symptom of rapid lying, B. Lynn bulges her eyeballs and says, "I don't know." The interior of the house endures extensive upheaval before the family treasure hunt spreads to the backyard. It is a lively game that requires much shouting out for clues and "I don't KNOW" responses, disturbing the neighborhood heathens who have the good fortune of remaining in bed on Sunday mornings.

B. Lynn's father is the winner of Huckle-Buckle-Shoe-Stalk: flinging her shoes to the ground he says, *She threw them in the goddam grapevines for chrissakes.* B. Lynn hopes he doesn't use that kind of language when he gets to church and has his conversation with God.

When they reach the front lawn of the Presbyterian Church, much to the consternation of other tardy parishioners, B. Lynn's father begins behaving like a man possessed by the Spirit. Swinging and shaking his left leg, he speaks rapidly in tongues:

Sonuvvagunleggoofmydammittohelllegfortheluvvachrise.

He looks down at B. Lynn, clinging to his leg like a small unpleasant dog with love on its mind, and uses the foot of his unencumbered leg to scrape at her fingers; she tumbles to the ground like a cicada shell dislodged from a tree, and she is ashamed of herself because everyone can see her Sunday underpants.

She is dragged into the Sunday school room howling like an unrepentant sinner heading to hades. Several minutes later she is hauled out of the Sunday school room and into the sanctuary of the church. Clutching B. Lynn's arm, the teacher leans over her mother's shoulder and hisses, *Never AGAIN.*

B. Lynn slumps in the pew next to her father, rigid with his displeasure of her, and runs her fingers over the gold letters on the Bible her gramma thought would make a fine birthday present. She doesn't understand why she's encouraged to read the Bible, filled with the stuff of nightmares, when she isn't allowed to watch The Twilight Zone on television.

Hearing the words *forgive us our trespasses*, B. Lynn leans forward and listens attentively because she is very interested in the subject of trespassing. She thinks of all the times Old Auntie Pagano, matriarch of the nest of Italians living in B. Lynn's neighborhood, has chased her out of her raspberry patch screeching and swinging her garden hoe like a saber. She doesn't know if she or Old Auntie is supposed to do the forgiving—and if neither of them does any forgiving, will they both go to hell?

Walking home after church, her mother steers her down the sidewalk with her index finger fingernail, creating stigmata on B. Lynn's back. She is poked into her bedroom and told she can stay in there for the rest of the day and think good and hard about her sins. B. Lynn lies on her bed and stares at the ceiling. She can't think of a single one.

Dazed
Day One

It is, in B. Lynn's judgment, a perfectly fine foot. It possesses five toes, the summer dirt has been scraped out from beneath the meticulously clipped toenails; the entire foot has been thoroughly scrubbed. There is a small blister forming on the back of the heel, caused by the despicable new Mary Janes, but that is a mere trifle. If anything, it resembles a fresh young squid placed, as it is, on a piece of newsprint, stripped of its secure nest of sock and shoe so that it is exposed and bare-naked for all her classmates to see.

The teacher, a kindly but muddled old woman, grunts down onto the floor and arranges herself on her hands and knees. She grasps a fat round green pencil and carefully draws an outline of the foot onto the newsprint. B. Lynn cautiously pats the back of the teacher's head. It is not a pleasant head to touch; there are uncomfortable looking pink patches of scalp peeping from the tightly coiffed gray hair.

Flushed from the unaccustomed position of being on her hand and knees, the teacher looks up and B. Lynn quietly asks her why she is making a spectacle of her foot. She replies that if she just tells her husband about this foot, he will never believe her. B. Lynn glances around at the gaggle of new classmates surrounding her, and hopes they also have abnormalities hiding in their shoes. The teacher staggers to her feet and grabs the back of the neck on B. Lynn's dress. She peers at the size tag inside the collar and utters a satisfied, *Huh.*

Confused and dispirited from her first day of kindergarten, B. Lynn goes home and tells her mother about the molestation of her foot and dress. She demands to know what's so unusual about the darned things. Her mother laughs, *They're little!*

They're so very LITTLE! You're wearing baby sizes, for crying out loud!

Day Two

Her classmates are privy to information she hasn't had enough time to process; everything happens too quickly. The teacher gives instructions and before she can even think, the other kids are already doing. She is an irrelevant dusty weed tumbling in a veldt of thundering rhinoceroses, as her classmates with their large ungainly bodies, rush past her to do the teacher's bidding. B. Lynn turns in a circle and says, "WHAT? What's going on? What're we doing? NOW what are we doing?" The best method of coping with this anxious-making situation is simply—very simply—imitate their behavior.

The rhinos have shuffled into a circle on the floor, so B. Lynn rushes over and elbows her way into the ring. They have their hands folded neatly in their laps and so she attempts this seemingly easy arrangement—but the fingers on her right hand refuse to allow Left Ring Finger and Left Baby Finger into the group. She sighs and hides her hands in the folds of her miserable dress.

B. Lynn looks doubtfully at the two sticks the teacher has given her. Harvey uses his to hit Georgie on the head. B. Lynn uses hers to whack Ramona's knee. These activities provoke sharp words from the teacher. B. Lynn glares at Harvey for giving her the wrong instructions.

The teacher claps and counts, ***ONE-two-THREE-four!*** The children dutifully tap their sticks. This is more like it. B. Lynn energetically bangs her sticks on the floor—she is Jerry Lee Lewis on drums. The teacher abruptly stops counting and clapping and yells, *To the beat! Tap to the BEAT!* B. Lynn looks up through hair that has fallen damply into her eyes from her assiduous drumming and says, "Beets? Who has beets?"

Day Three

She holds in her lap a wondrous thing. B. Lynn jiggles impatiently in her chair waiting her turn at Show and Tell, inwardly sneering at the commonplace doll Rebecca displays, Joey's postcard from Rock City Park; Deborah's pop-bead necklace.

What she has defies the imagination, and her hands tremble with excitement when the teacher calls her name. She silently holds her Show aloft—there isn't much to tell— and waits expectantly for the class's reaction. They gaze amazed and dumbfounded. The teacher clears her throat and says, *Why... yes. That is certainly a very nice thing.*

B. Lynn happily lowers the Show she has artfully created and looks into the small glass jar filled with water. Floating exotically within is the head of a rubber snake. The jar slips from her still trembling fingers and crashes onto the floor. Her Show becomes nothing more than a dumb old rubber snakehead, that she had yanked off the rest of the snake, lying in a small puddle of water and shattered glass.

Day Four

It is raining; she is late. Marvin, the boy who lives next door, has the job of walking ahead of B. Lynn to clear the sidewalks of worms—but he is staying home from school today, happily ensconced in bed with a cold in his head.

B. Lynn clutches the front of her raincoat and walks on her tiptoes. She finds a worm-free island of sidewalk and stands there a moment to rest her toes and steady her nerves. A fat glistening earthworm pokes its revolting swaying head out of the grass and glides directly in her path. B. Lynn clenches the front of her raincoat more tightly and hyperventilates.

Head reeling, her limbs are weak. She scrunches her eyes but quickly snaps them back wide open. She can't watch; she has to watch as the worm stretches itself long and skinny in front of her. It is a horrific situation: surrounded by worms, she is trapped.

Eventually, some of them wiggle back into the grass, finding the sidewalk inhospitable to their needs. B. Lynn tiptoes, clutches, rests and hyperventilate the rest of the way to school. The two-block walk is a forty minute journey through worm hell.

The school corridor is so silent and deserted B. Lynn wonders if everyone else got to stay home because of the worms. The kindergarten door is closed, tight-lipped and frowning. She reaches for the doorknob and discovers it is placed a few inches higher than her outstretched hand, making it necessary to jump and hit at the underside of the knob with the tips of her fingers.

She is momentarily distracted by noise and laughter coming from the open room across the hall, and turns around to see who the heck is having fun in school. It is the four-year-old kindergarten class. Although only four-years-old herself, she is disdainful of the room full of babies. Frantically—she doesn't want to get put in there for failing Introduction to Door Opening—she resumes her efforts to grab the doorknob until her teacher notices it is jiggling around for no apparent reason and opens the door.

Day Five

She refuses to use it because her classmates will know why she is using it. But it has been another distressing morning of uncertainty and behinded-ness and B. Lynn, against her more refined sensibilities, finds she has no choice but to use it.

She asks for permission to enter the small closet-like room just large enough to accommodate a toilet, tightly wedged between the walls, and quietly closes the door. There isn't a lock and it seems a mighty thin door to conceal her from all the kids right on the other side. B. Lynn believes it is indecent that kindergarteners are made to use a bathroom that is right in the classroom, when there is a laboratory down the hall that would give a person some privacy. She sits straddled on the toilet, a precarious position because the front part of the seat is missing—she doesn't want her legs to touch the spattered white porcelain—and tries to not make any noise.

Uneasily balanced, she wipes herself with a fistful of small squares of paper that feel like flattened blocks of shredded wheat. Jumping off her perch, she stretches over the toilet to push the flusher; the silver handle is just out of reach. She leans farther over the toilet, loses her balance and slams her hands down on the back of the seat, just in time to save her head from plunging into the yellow water.

Squeezing between the wall and toilet, she flails her hand in the direction of the flusher until the teacher pounds on the door and yells, *Are you okay in there?* B. Lynn stays silent. The teacher flings open the door and there they are: the whole class peering into the bathroom like a bunch of rubes at a sideshow.

Not about to let everyone know what she's been doing, B. Lynn plants herself firmly in front of the toilet and whispers in the teacher's ear. The teacher pats her head, pushes her aside and performs the flush. As she is slinking back to her desk, the teacher yells, *WASH YOUR HANDS for goodness sake.*

B. Lynn has eagerly anticipated this moment all week: Friday, three o'clock P.M.—

but she is not in the mood for celebration; she is in a black funk. Walking, head down, she glumly enjoys the destruction she is causing her Mary Janes by dragging her toes along the sidewalk. She is oblivious of the kids racing past her shrieking and shoving, insane with excitement about the weekend, because she is intent on scuffing and thinking. She can't decide which is more ridiculous: school or herself.

Over the River

B. Lynn peels her bare legs from the clear vinyl seat covers that have kept her glued in place for the past hour, and crawls out of the family car. Hoisting up her dress, she rubs the backs of her legs where red welts are forming and then pulls at the elastic waistband of her underpants that are cutting a hot belt around her belly. Her mother yanks her dress back down to her knees and she feels like a fatted calf: branded and trussed in her Sunday outfit, prickly and too tight under her arms.

She gazes despondently at Gramma waiting for them on her front porch, and then trails behind her parents and sister, watching as they receive reasonable kisses on their cheeks. When it is her turn for the kiss she ducks and feints left—but Gramma surprises her with the speed and dexterity of a cobra: coiling down, she clutches B. Lynn's chin in her knotty fist and fastens her whiskery lips directly over her right ear. She gives it a big wet resounding–*Mmmwaa!* B. Lynn feels as if most of her brains have just been sucked out through her auditory canal. She staggers into her grandmother's house half-deaf and depressed.

Sagging dull and stupid next to her mother on the sofa in Gramma's living room, B. Lynn struggles to stay conscious. She is overcome with oxygen deprivation caused from cigarette smoke, her mother's Sunday perfume, and kitchen stove fumes because Gramma can't remember to light the burners with a match after she turns on the gas. She briefly wonders if they will get to eat dinner before the combination of gas fumes and glowing-tipped cigarettes blow everyone out the roof, scattering their arms and legs all over Cattaraugus County.

Her head rolls and knocks into her mother, who knifes her in the ribs with her elbow and hisses, *We didn't come here to sleep. Sit up and talk to your grandmother.* B. Lynn jerks upright and peers at Gramma through eyes, raw and bleary.

"Hi Gramma." Gramma looks at her and shrivels her lips as if she's sucking lemon juice through a straw. B. Lynn is perfectly aware she disgusts her grandmother. As the last potential grandchild to carry on the family name, Gramma is personally insulted that B. Lynn was born with female paraphernalia. B. Lynn wonders if Gramma knows she is also disgusted and personally insulted that she was born with female paraphernalia.

Hoping "Hi Gramma" was enough to fulfill the conversation mandates, she flops back into her stupor.

Floating through a fog of half-consciousness, B. Lynn realizes she is so thirsty her tongue feels as if it has swollen to the size of the Goodyear blimp. She slips off the sofa and casually walks into the kitchen. Looking around to make sure she is alone, she silently opens the refrigerator door, grabs the milk bottle and starts to give it a good shake. Gramma spooks up behind her—*B. LYNN!* B. Lynn shoves the bottle back into the refrigerator and slams the door.

Shaking a bottle of pasteurized milk is a crime comparable to peeing on the living room carpet. Gramma skims the cream, floating at the top of the bottle, and saves it to put in her coffee. She makes her grandchildren drink the remaining blue-tinged watery substance with their dinner. B. Lynn's taste buds refuse to accept it. She stares at the blank white face of the refrigerator door until she hears Gramma turn and walk out of the kitchen.

There is a battered tin ladle hanging over the kitchen sink; it is the communal drinking cup because it is against the rules to dirty a glass for a lousy drink of water. B. Lynn has been told that her father, aunt and uncles, drank from it when they were children and it makes her sick to her stomach to think

43

about all those years of built-up spit—and she has seen phlegmy old Uncle Robert drink from the nasty thing. Also, the water at Gramma's house tastes like swimming pool water. She slumps back to the living room, her tongue gummed to the roof of her mouth. Dinner is a tedious affair. B. Lynn straddles a stool leaking straw stuffing, that rankles the vinyl seat cover injuries on the backs of her legs. Sucking the moisture out of a piece of celery, she listens to her parents shout back and forth with Gramma. They yell because Gramma is as deaf as a ping pong ball—although B. Lynn's mother says, *She hears what she wants to hear.* Their voices ricochet in her still ringing right ear. After dinner, the sight of her father washing dishes fascinates B. Lynn. He becomes a different person when he is in his childhood home. He even responds to an unfamiliar name: Julian. B. Lynn knows his real name is Ed—or Gib. Because he washes dishes and answers to the wrong name, she thinks maybe her father shares her terror of his mother.

On the ride home, B. Lynn sprawls in the back seat of the car bellowing a round of songs because she's pretty sure her family enjoys listening to her. As she is about to launch into a family favorite, she stops and thinks: *Who the heck would love going to their gramma's house so much they'd write the ridiculous song, Over the River and Through the Woods to Grandmother's House We Go!*

Solitaire

Lying in bed, B. Lynn stretches her foot to her mouth and sucks her big toe. It is desultory sucking; she lost her taste for the appendage months ago. She has continued the awkward practice because it makes her father be happy to say, *B. Lynn, that's a marvelous feet feat,* and she would suck on her nose if it made her father be happy.

The proximity of her leg to her eyes reminds her that she has an interesting science project on her knee. Spitting out her toe, she pulls her knee to her face so that she can more closely examine the scab that is squatting there like a small brown toad. The scab is a curiosity, the development of which, confounding. Monitoring the thing for the last several days, B. Lynn has been trying to determine the source of the scab's conception. She has formulated two hypotheses: it has grown out of her scrape and taken root on her knee like a little patch of fungus, or it has been cultivated by something that is airborne—like pollination.

Idly running her fingers over the rough surface of the scab, her mind drifts until it snags on a horrific thought: Ramona at school told her jungle people get maggots in their scrapes because they don't know about Band-Aides—and that was a hateful bit of information Ramona gave her because she knows B. Lynn has a scrape and also a particular aversion to things that wiggle.

After reviewing the recent activities of her knee, she is fairly certain it has escaped maggot infestation. She hasn't done any kneeling to investigate small animal carcasses for several weeks, nor has she witnessed any Blue Bottle Flies swarming her leg.

It occurs to her there might be such a thing as scab-gnats. There could be scab-gnats flying around, scouting for fresh scrapes to land on so they can use them as nurseries. The bumpy topography of the scab could be an indication that it isn't really a scab at all—but a clutch of scab-gnat eggs that will give birth to maggots right on the private property of her knee. B. Lynn searches her body for raw flesh and discovers some on her left ankle; she shoves her feet under her blanket in case some scab-gnats try to claim squatters' rights.

Staring at the ceiling, she notices there are two blurred cracks when the night before there had been only one perfectly cracked crack. She realizes her troubling optical condition might have been caused by the close inspection of her knee. In a blind panic, B. Lynn rapidly flutters her eyelashes and rolls her eyeballs until they ache so they won't get stuck looking at each other for the rest of their lives.

Deborah at school wears a patch over one eye because it is crossed, and B. Lynn wouldn't mind if just one of her own eyes struck a pigeon-toed position for a little while. It is a fine trick Deborah has, crossing one eye without the other following suit—it is an amazing display of eyeball dexterity—a singular talent she would also like to achieve.

B. Lynn is able to wag her baby toe back and forth all by itself, but it is a skill that goes largely unappreciated at school. A demonstration of her ability would require the removal of her shoe and sock and she is not inclined to remove her shoe and sock, exposing the vulnerability of her naked sock-puckered foot to the whole class.

The neighborhood kids are allowed to observe the solitary movements of her baby toe because they are a competitive group and they always attempt to duplicate this phenomenon. As a result, they are all familiar with the spectacle of each other's feet and thus no longer feel the necessity to remark upon them.

Holding a hand over her right eye to see what Deborah sees, she only sees what she always sees. She covers her other eye as well, and doesn't see anything. B. Lynn wonders if both Deborah's eyes were crossed—would she have to wear two patches?—if that were the case she would be blind.

B. Lynn keeps her eyes closed to experience blindness. She sticks her fingers in her ears to experience deafness. She is now experiencing blindness and deafness. It is surprising that even though her ears are stoppered, she still has the ability to hear her own thoughts.

It would be interesting to experience blindness, deafness and dumbness like Helen Keller. Making her tongue stand still, B. Lynn discovers her throat can still make noises because there is clear passage for sounds to escape. So Helen Keller might not have been stupid after all—she may have simply swallowed her tongue and it was hanging upside down blocking her throat. B. Lynn wonders if anyone ever bothered to look in her mouth. Also, if people had thought to put their ears against Helen Keller's neck they might have been able to hear her tongue talking.

Impatient with blindness and deafness, and suffering stiff tongue fatigue, B. Lynn raises her fists and holds them in front of her face. Pointer suddenly springs out of the finger nest and swivels around looking for some finger friends. He yells, *Where is everybody.*

Other Pointer pops up and says, *Here I am.* Pointer and Other Pointer bob their heads and have an agreeable conversation until Middle and Other Middle curl out of the nest to see what's going on. The Pointers hate the Middles—they think they are the finger bosses because they are taller than everybody else and also B. Lynn's mother says they're rude when they play outside by themselves.

The Pointers say to the Middles, *Get out of here.*

The Middles say, *Make us.* They say, *You can't tell us what to do this is our hand too and we can stay here if we want.* The Pointers and the Middles begin poking and pushing each other and then the Ringies come out to join the fight, dragging the Pinkies along with them. The Ringies always have to babysit the Pinkies because the Pinkies are big babies and refuse to stay in the nest without them.

Now everyone is outside—except the Thumbs. They are short and fat so nobody ever wants to play with them. The two finger gangs glare at each other for a minute and then Pointer smacks Other Middle on the head. The Ringies hold each other in headlocks and the Pinkies stand on the sidelines calling everybody nasty names—they're small, but they have really big mouths.

Other Pointer suddenly flies up and deals a forceful jab to B. Lynn's left cheek. The fingers quickly leave off fighting and silently turn to look at B. Lynn, wondering what kind of hell he's going to catch. B. Lynn yells at Thumb to come out and help Middle give Other Pointer a good flicking. Thumb and Middle administer three solid snaps and then Thumb hastily retreats back into the nest before someone starts picking on him.

The fingers resume tangling and wrestling until they look like a mess of earthworms wriggling on the ends of B. Lynn's hands; she thrusts them under her blankets and waits for everyone to calm down and start acting like normal fingers.

B. Lynn's mother, walking down the hallway, pauses by B. Lynn's open bedroom door. She quietly observes her daughter, and then says, *What are you doing.*

Rolling her head on her pillow so she can look at her mother, she replies, "Playing with myself."

Her mother stiffens and hisses, *Get yourself out of that bed right this minute young lady and go wash your filthy hands. Good GOD.*

On the Move

B. Lynn looks up at the bland face of the clock on the wall. Her heart stumbles. She folds her arms on her desk, lowers her head, slowly twists her neck and raises her elbow. She peeks out from under her armpit and looks straight into the narrowed eyes of her nemesis. She feels like a chipmunk trapped in its hidey-hole by a rattlesnake. B. Lynn sighs and looks back at the clock.

She is all too familiar with the wretched girl in her classroom who sits and stares at the back of her head all day until she feels as if there are cooties scratching around on her neck and in her hair. The girl lives on the other side of her back fence. She is part of the tumbling rat's nest of squalling filthy urchins who are daily ushered—with screams and threats issued from a huge harridan of a mother named Gert—into their yard of trampled dirt and weeds.

B. Lynn's mother has warned her not to talk to these children—*and don't TOUCH them, for crying out loud.* B. Lynn has never been inclined to touch them, for crying out loud. Although she is not particularly particular about dirt herself, these children, scabbed and gooey-nosed with bathtub rings circling their necks, are beyond even B. Lynn's liberal standards of cleanliness. And the rank smell of pee-soaked underpants wafting about them like yellow smog is inducement enough to keep her well back from the fence.

Demoralized chicken wire keeps the children caged in their yard, and B. Lynn has spent many idle summer afternoons sitting in her sandbox observing and wondering about the peculiar lives of these children. She has watched them clamber around on their derelict swing set that also holds them prisoner: when they tire of clambering and cluster at their fence to stare

50

back at B. Lynn—the only other source of entertainment available to them—Gert thrusts her big moon of a head out the window and bellows, *Get on those sons-a-bitchin swings and SWING! You get back on those mothafuckin swings and SHUT UP!* B. Lynn reels at the free use of the forbidden words *shut up*, and she stores the other unfamiliar words in her brain for further investigation.

In addition to passively observing the interesting spectacle of the neglected children over the fence, B. Lynn—along with other Prescott Street kids—has also indulged in many pleasurable hours screeching colorful descriptions of their appearance and personalities. Behind the safety of the fence, B. Lynn becomes a pack member of howling wolves, snarling with bloodlust and tearing at the fabric of lives already tattered.

The oldest girl reminds B. Lynn of Wendy the Witch in her Little Lulu comic books and she has taken advantage of every opportunity to call her Wendy the Witch. She is delighted the girl's name also happens to be Wendy.

In return for all the pleasantries exchanged over the summer, Wendy the Witch, now unfenced and loose in B. Lynn's classroom, has made it her business to chase B. Lynn home from school every miserable day. B. Lynn is not unduly concerned about Wendy's plans for her if she is caught—she just doesn't want to *TOUCH her, for crying out loud.*

Her heart now dancing a complicated jitterbug, B. Lynn looks back at the clock. She inches forward in her chair and cracks her knuckles. Five—four—three—two—one—the bell rings and she is on her feet and out the classroom door. She is in the hallway—head down, butting and shoving through tangles of kids. She bursts out the school doors—she's on the move and moving fast—feet pounding the pavement with Wendy the Witch right on her heels.

Six-Foot Feat

B. Lynn's father mutters and scribbles furiously on graph paper. He curses, throws his scribblings down on the dining room floor and starts again. B. Lynn asks him what he is doing and he says, *FIGURING*. She gathers up some of the discarded papers and examines them.

Because she is only four years old, B. Lynn hasn't yet been introduced to the confounding subject of mathematics and so she isn't able to make sense of the numbers. She doesn't know that never in her life will she be able to make sense of the numbers.

***

Her father has made a huge mess in the back yard and there is a circus of neighbors in the front yard. B. Lynn runs breathlessly back and forth through the house. She looks out the kitchen window at her father standing next to his mess in the backyard and then races to the front screen door to scowl at all the people who are having themselves a good old time, gawking and whispering on her property.

A bark of laughter occasionally pierces the air, followed by a staccato string of Italian because B. Lynn and her family live right in the middle of Fair Field's "Little Italy." They are saying her father has lost his mind, he's gone off the deep end—*he is LO-CO, man*—and they roll their eyes as they twirl their fingers next to their temples.

Her mother snorts and says they don't know a damned thing about anything because they wear blue collars when they go to work. B. Lynn can tell by the tone of her mother's voice that she finds the color of their collars offensive. She and her sister have several blouses with blue collars, and she worries that maybe they shouldn't be wearing them out in public and risk having people think they don't know a damned thing about anything.

She doesn't often share her mother's opinions, but in this they agree: they don't like the neighbors' attitudes one little bit. B. Lynn would like to get outside and twist their fingers backwards, but she is contained in the house. Her father has dug a hole in their back yard big enough to bury the entire neighborhood and her mother firmly believes that, if given the opportunity, B. Lynn will promptly head straight for the hole and tumble in. Her head will crack open and hers will be the first body to christen the yawning, ready-made grave. Frustrated, B. Lynn kicks the front door and displays her tongue.

Although she doesn't believe the excessive rumors flying around about her father's mental instability, B. Lynn is a little uneasy about his behavior. He is a quiet man and shy, normally fading into her mother's formidable shadow. Now, he's exposed in full living color and she worries that under the glare of their neighbors' inspections, he might shrivel up and wilt like a dandelion plucked out of the ground and tossed in the hot sun.

One day, her father brings home The Guys from Work. B. Lynn is relieved none of them have risked her mother's disgust by wearing shirts with blue collars, but she is appalled that her father is letting people from work see his huge mess. She pushes her face against the kitchen window, prepared to break through the glass and yank their fingers around if they start laughing at him. They do start laughing, but only because they are consuming large quantities of beer and clumping around in big rubber boots. She hopes they don't think they're going to be doing any fishing in that big old muddy hole, because there is nothing down there but bait.

The house trembles and B. Lynn's father and The Guys from Work cheer. She dashes to the dining room window just in time to see a cement truck lumbering down her driveway.

***

B. Lynn gazes down into clear blue water. Her father has built her a swimming pool. He is not completely satisfied with his project; there won't be a diving board because too much cement was delivered and so the pool is only six feet deep. And the magazine plans said it would cost five hundred dollars to build and it cost a THOUSAND. Also, the walls are lumpy. But B. Lynn knows it is one mighty fine pool.

She drags her eyes away from the water to look across the swimming pool at her father looking at her. He is undamaged and still in full living color.

Sleep

B. Lynn clings to the edge of the mattress like a barnacle stuck on the side of a sinking ship. It is a precarious position—uncomfortable, too—but it is as close as she can get to the relative safety of the open bedroom door and still technically remain in bed. She is tense, coiled, and prepared for flight. When the wolf that lives under her bed raises his grizzled snarling snout, she is ready to catapult out of her bedroom and down the hall to her parents' room.

B. Lynn stares at the dim yellow light in the hallway. She blinks once, twice. Her eyes wander and then freeze on her toy vacuum cleaner. With its battery-powered light and whirring motor sound it is a marvel of technology, and B. Lynn knows when she falls asleep it will snap to life and begin careening around her bedroom. It will bang into the furniture and zoom back and forth next to her side of the bed, pinning her in the glare of its rolling headlamp eye. It will become a crazed mindless toy out of control.

"Daddy? DAD!"

Her father charges out of his bedroom and breathlessly leans into her room, supporting himself on the doorjamb. *What's wrong?*

"You forgot to put my vacuum in the closet."

He looks at B. Lynn for a moment, and then grabs the vacuum by its handle and flings it into the closet. *Go to sleep.*

She is satisfied that the treacherous thing has been adequately contained until she notices there is a flagrant violation of the Safety Code. "Dad! The closet door isn't shut all the way."

He turns and, with one rigid finger, nudges the door a quarter of an inch to make the latch click solidly into place. *Go to sleep.*

She resumes her vigil and stares at the light in the hallway. A wave of terror suddenly rolls up her legs and whirlpools in her stomach. It sloshes upward, knocks her heart around and then gushes out the top of her head, leaving her lips numb and her feet dead as tree stumps. Dennis is missing. Without releasing her grip on the edge of the mattress, she scoots onto her stomach and frantically scrambles her right hand around on the empty and dangerous side of the bed. "Dad? DAD!" Her father's shadow looms large in the doorway, blocking the light in the hallway. "I can't find my Dennis."

After giving the ceiling some consideration her father leans over, grunts, and blindly swipes his hand on the floor, just missing the wolf under the bed. He grabs Dennis the Menace by his vinyl cowlick and tosses him in B. Lynn's direction. She snatches the doll and tightens her grasp on the mattress.

Go to sleep.

The house settles and groans and B. Lynn's eyeballs are stuck wide open. She stares at the light in the hallway. A pile of dirty clothes in the corner of her bedroom distracts her focus on the light—are they MOVING? Eyes riveted, she watches and yes—they most certainly ARE moving. "Dad! I need a drink of water!"

Her father shuffles from the bathroom in his tired pajamas and silently holds out a glass of tepid water. B. Lynn is slightly revolted by the toothpaste-spattered bathroom glass. She would much prefer kitchen water. But she takes a tentative sip and peers over the rim of the glass at her father. "Thank you."

Go to sleep.

Her vision blurs and her breathing slows. But what the HECK was THAT noise? Heart pounding, she listens and hears it again... the WOLF! "Dad? Dad! DA-"

FOR THE LUVA GOD—GO TO SLEEP!

B. Lynn clutches the blanket and Dennis under her chin with one sweaty fist; hangs onto the edge of the mattress with the other. She stares at the light in the hallway. The vacuum cleaner bumps in the closet. The wolf under the bed shifts restlessly and yawns.

Love-Hate Affairs

B. Lynn rolls around on the living room floor and howls until her crowbar wielding father sends her upstairs to her bedroom—because *there is ENOUGH RACKET going on in here for chrissakes.*

Lying on her bed she listens to the shriek of splintering wood in the living room; she shrieks in return and kicks her feet. Her sister pounds up the stairs and stands in B. Lynn's bedroom doorway, looking at her like she's some kind of junk she found on the bottom of her shoe.

Mom wants to know if you've completely lost your mind, Soozie-Bells says.

B. Lynn glares at her sister through hair stringy and damp and says, "He's hurting them."

They're JUST BOOKCASES, Soozie-Bells snorts. B. Lynn pulls her pillow over her face and moans. She hates her mother for making her father hack the built-in twin bookcases into shards of sad naked wood—just to make more room for furniture. She thinks of the confusion and hurt feelings the bookcases' are suffering from their abrupt dismemberment and she shrieks again. Her sister says, *Good grief,* and B. Lynn hates her sister.

***

Pressing her face against the window, B. Lynn's raining nose makes a glistening trail of wet on the glass. She slaps the window pane, turns, and runs through the house and out the back door.

She is too late; the faithful Pontiac is already rolling backward down the driveway on its death march to the used car lot. The car gazes at her through dejected head lights and B.

58

Lynn screams and stomps her foot. She runs down the driveway until her father flaps his hand at her to get back. Collapsing in the dirt and gravel, she keens for the car that has to leave home without her kiss goodbye. Her father beeps the horn as he starts down the street, and B. Lynn hates him. Mary Catherine from next door walks out of her house and asks why she's crying about getting a new car, and she hates Mary Catherine, too.

***

She tries to ignore the arrogant bicycle standing next to the Christmas tree and hopes it isn't meant for her, because she already has a bike and she likes it just fine. B. Lynn's anxious parents look at her not looking at the bike, and she looks at her sister who is also looking at her not looking at the bike. B. Lynn sighs. The bike is meant for her.

She feels the heavy weight of expectancy in the room, so she walks over and looks at the bike, its handlebars curved in a complacent sneer. She lightly touches the slick handlebars and remembers the warm patina of rust on her old bike. She knows her old bike's heart is going to break when it finds out it won't be taking her for rides anymore.

Tears threaten to clog her throat and plug her nose when she thinks of her old bike standing alone in the cold dark garage, while this unfriendly stranger is in the warm house having Christmas with the family.

B. Lynn can feel her parents' eyes poking her in the back and it makes her sad that she hates the Christmas present they picked out especially for her. She turns to them and says, "I LOVE it!"

***

Puddy doesn't want to be called Ranger, but B. Lynn wants her to be called Ranger. She actually would like a horse called Ranger but she has to make do with her old dog called Puddy. B. Lynn believes Puddy is an embarrassing name for her dog. She doesn't like that her dog has been named after puddles of pee. Ranger is a heroic boy dog name, although Puddy is a girl.

B. Lynn clutches Puddy's collar and drags her across the kitchen floor: "C'mon Ranger–good boy Ranger, let's go." Puddy's feet skitter on the linoleum. B. Lynn swings her around and slides her back across the kitchen floor and says, "Here we go, Ranger–good DOG!"

When she decides Puddy has been sufficiently trained to respond to her new name, B. Lynn releases her collar and walks a few feet away. She turns, squats, and claps her hands: "Come here Ranger! C'mon Ranger! Good boy! Ranger... COME!"

Puddy gazes glumly at B. Lynn, and then relaxes herself into a heap on the floor. B. Lynn's patience is used up with her girl dog named Puddy, so reaches out and smacks her on the nose. The unexpected violence to her nose makes Puddy bewildered and B. Lynn shocked and weak with remorse. She throws herself onto Puddy, wraps her arms around her neck and sobs, "You're a good girl, Puddy–Puddy-Pup I love you– Oh my GOSH, PUDDY!" She assaults her with kisses and rubs her face in her fur with promises of doggie treats and ham bones and a ride in the car—and the only person she hates is herself.

Some Kind of Time

It is a sullen day of November chill; it is another Sunday at Gramma's. Standing on the front sidewalk of Gramma's house, B. Lynn sighs, depression settling over her like a mantle of soot. She thrusts her hand inside the top of her coat and down into her dress. She scratches her chest and armpits where the miserable dress worries her skin.

Her three cousins silently watch her scratch, their mouths gaping so that they look like the 'Toss Miss Beanbag in the Hole' game at the carnival. They are afraid of B. Lynn, and dismayed that her behavior included them in the ejection from Gramma's house until dinner time. They don't harbor any familial affection for her, and B. Lynn despises the sight of them. Bonnie suggests they go down into Gramma's basement and get out the old wicker baby buggy. They could push it up and down the street and pretend they're a family taking their baby for a Sunday stroll! She looks wide-eyed at her brothers and licks her lips; she is a lip-licker that comes of breathing through her mouth that she holds open in case there is an opportunity to plunge food into it.

B. Lynn knows that eating is a bad habit to get into. Whenever she wants a little snack, her mother says, *Do you want to get fat like your cousin Bonnie?* B. Lynn thinks there might be some benefits to getting fat like her cousin Bonnie. Last summer at the family reunion, there was a race for all the kids and B. Lynn won it—she WON it. But Bonnie got the prize and everybody cheered because she managed to FINISH the race. Also, she can eat whenever and whatever she wants without any worries because she is already fat.

Making a noise about Bonnie's baby buggy idea makes Bonnie shut her mouth. Petey, talking fast because he needs to keep his tongue prepared to catch the steady flow of unpleasant matter sliding from his nose, says maybe they could swing on the swings over by the old airplane factory.

B. Lynn thinks about that lone rusted swing set, isolated in a field of weeds behind the empty factory. She imagines one of the swings swaying back and forth without a passenger. The place stirs uneasy feelings of nameless terror. No, she won't swing.

Bonnie starts babbling again about the old wicker baby buggy and B. Lynn yells, "I said NO!" She has seen faded pictures of Gramma pushing two little girls in that buggy—and they both died. She thinks fooling around with that old buggy is a risky business because dying might be contagious.

Patrick sighs heavily through his open mouth. He can't breathe through his nose because he has noids growing inside it. He puts his hands on his waist, thrusts his left hip out to the side, taps his right foot, and rolls his eyes. He thinks playing with the buggy is a marvelous idea.

B. Lynn squints at Patrick. He doesn't act like the other boys she plays with. She can't figure out what's different about him, but he acts an awful lot like Uncle Robert—and she can't figure out what's different about him, either.

Petey says maybe they could take a walk on the train tracks. B. Lynn yells that people's feet get stuck in train tracks—doesn't he know that? And then trains come along and chop off people's legs so they have to use their hands to push themselves around on little boards with wheels like people in the sideshow at the fair—doesn't he KNOW THAT? Petey stares at B. Lynn and flicks his tongue under his nose.

Uncle Harvey, the cousins' father, pops his head out Gramma's front door and says it's time for dinner. He wags his eyebrows at B. Lynn and she feels as if someone just blew cold air on the back of her neck.

B. Lynn's mother says Uncle Harvey is slimy. B. Lynn has never noticed any glistening on his skin, but he does remind her of Oil Can Harry in cartoons. Oil Can doesn't talk, and he is devious. Manipulating his face into various expressions, he tricks beautiful ladies into being his friend. Then he ties them up on railroad tracks.

It wouldn't surprise B. Lynn in the least if Uncle Harvey tied somebody up on the railroad tracks, because he acts just like Oil Can Harry. Uncle Harvey smiles without showing his teeth and her mother says it isn't a smile—it's a leer. He wiggles his eyebrows up and down, and whenever B. Lynn gets in trouble for something she didn't do he makes his eyes big, says, *Oh my,* and then puts his fingertips on his mouth.

Following her cousins into Gramma's house, B. Lynn is already sick to her stomach because she knows Uncle Robert is going to pretend to cough and choke on phlegm so she won't be able to eat anymore and he can have her dessert.

On the drive home, B. Lynn's father calls into the backseat, *Did you have a nice time?* She looks at the back of his sad, anxious head as he peers at her through the rearview mirror. His defeated shoulders and tight grip on the steering wheel give her a pretty good idea about the kind of time he had. Sliding her eyes to her mute mother and sister, she realizes they aren't going to say one word about the kind of time they had.

She thinks about her father's niece and nephews with their gaping mouth-holes and considers his brother, Uncle Robert— she can't figure out what's different about him. She imagines having a sister married to Oil Can Harry.

Her father moves his gaze from the rearview mirror and stares hard at the road. B. Lynn, still looking at the back of his poor tired head, replies, "YES!"

You Better Watch Out

Oh! The glory of it all! The Christmas tree stands tall in the living room, resplendent in its finery of paper chains and spent flash bulbs, carefully decorated with liberal amounts of paste and glitter. The glowing paper Star of Sweden dangles from the top of the doorframe between the living and dining rooms. The small bulb within the star is powered from a brown extension cord that snakes down the white woodwork and along the baseboards until it joins five other cords, piggy-backed and greedily sucking electricity from a single outlet.

Sitting grandly in the center of the dining room table is a gingerbread house, only slightly listing and nibbled upon. A green plastic wreath, with a plastic candle and flame, is scotch-taped to the front window; fat orange, blue, and green lights have been untangled, cursed upon and haphazardly strung around the front porch.

But the most spectacular sight of all is the stately cardboard fireplace. Nestled in the cardboard logs is a bulb that burns brightly behind orange cellophane. A small fan rotates in front of the bulb to create the illusion of flames, merrily dancing.

B. Lynn sits on the floor in front of the fireplace enjoying the coziness of a good crackling fire. She warms her toes on the orange cellophane and furtively gobbles Christmas cookies and candy. She studies the fireplace. The logistics of the thing confound her. She has been assured that—yes, indeed, Santa does come down the chimney and through the fireplace. B. Lynn has no great knowledge of engineering, but she is perfectly aware the chimney on the house is not directly situated over this fireplace. She also knows there is not an opening behind it. Does he come through the WALL?

The matter weighs heavily on B. Lynn's mind and sits restlessly in her stomach. She pushes her school Christmas concert crown, created with empty toilet paper rolls wrapped with crepe paper, so that they might resemble candles, back on her head and gives the problem further consideration.

Her mother calls out from the kitchen, *You better watch out... He knows when you've been naughty!* B. Lynn gags on a cookie crumb and shudders. Her mother has been singing this uncomfortable song a little too often. She hopes her good behavior during the past week is enough to negate the multitude of crimes she has committed in the past year. She wishes she had had the sense to think about Christmas way back in May. Candy and cookies roll like an ocean wave in her stomach.

On Christmas Eve, B. Lynn sprawls on her father's lap gazing at the Christmas tree. Her head aches to the rhythm of her pounding heart; she is nearly swooning with the onset of a cookie coma. Every nerve in her body is thrumming with excitement and terror as she has visions of Santa lurching around the living room, the cardboard fireplace clinging to his back while he crams her stocking full of switches and coal.

Her mother dances into the living room gaily singing, *He knows when you've been naughty, he knows if you've been good or bad!* Candy and cookies shift ominously in B. Lynn's stomach.

And so it is on this night she offers her traditional Christmas gift, her generous contribution to the holiday festivities. Struggling to get off her father's lap, she leans over, opens her mouth and decorates her dog, Puddy-Pup, lying on the floor beneath her feet, with bountiful amounts of chocolate and peppermint, walnuts and raisins. And so it is on this night her mother offers her solitary prayer in recognition of the holy occasion—*JESUSMARYANDJOSEPH!*

Oh! The glory of it all!

A Small Thing

They resemble parentheses that have tipped over into frowns: thin black marks of punctuation painted firmly above her eyes.

B. Lynn's mother claims she lost her left eyebrow in 1932, during an incident with a car. She and her brother, Junior, had just been released from their murky schoolroom that was rank with the smell of leek perspiration oozing from the pores of their classmates. It was the Great Depression and the children, given the choices of *nothing to eat* or *nothing to eat but leeks,* invariably chose the latter.

Reeling with fresh air intoxication, she and Junior thoughtlessly dashed into the street and immediately encountered a radiator grill. They were briefly introduced to the under-workings of an automobile and then the heels of their feet were snatched up by the rear bumper.

The driver of the car, perhaps reeling with his own choice of intoxication, was unaware of their predicament and continued on his way. The children were dragged down the street like a couple of forgotten tin cans from a wedding celebration.

Eventually, contorting with the natural elasticity of children, they were able to unhinge themselves from the bumper. During her release, the exhaust pipe made a passing comment to her face, which resulted in the erasure of her left eyebrow. She decided to pluck out the other so they would baldly match. Junior managed to keep his eyebrows intact and it was thought he was left unscathed, until he developed an anxious tic which was attributed to eyebrow survivor's guilt.

Ultimately, her life comes to revolve around her nude forehead; it holds her hostage. Unwilling to leave the house and expose her deformity to the public, she always announces, *I have to go put on my eyebrows.* Her husband and daughters, ready for an excursion, mill aimlessly about in the front foyer as they wait for her to complete her face.

A tiny pointed brush, blackened from a small tray of charcoal-like substance, softened with her spit and the scrubbing around of the brush, is used for the application of her eyebrows. Leaning in toward the bureau mirror, her tongue creeping out of her mouth just enough to give her the appearance of having three lips, she carefully reproduces the missing hairs. She seems to take great satisfaction in the results of her work; perhaps the process nurtures some vague artistic longing.

Her left eyebrow is a rogue, having the ability to move itself up and down without the slightest regard for the right eyebrow, which might have been planning a different activity. B. Lynn is wary of the dreadful eyebrow and uses it as a barometer to gauge the vagaries of her mother's temperament.

She is reassured when the eyebrow is idle, which indicates she isn't causing any feelings of maternal aggravation. Spasmodic flickering means her mother is considering aggravation. When the eyebrow remains in a raised position—a position that can be held for such a great length of time B. Lynn wonders at the muscular strength of her forehead—she knows she has skidded over the boundaries of aggravation and has become ensnared in the barbed wire of her mother's disposition.

The raising and holding generally occur in social situations when her mother prefers to let her eyebrow be in charge of discipline. B. Lynn is chilled if the left eyebrow yells, *What the HELL do you think you're doing.* She is paralyzed if it threatens, *Wait until I get you home.*

It is a small movement, the lifting of the eyebrow, but it holds up a mighty weight of dire implications.

Pain in the Ass

It is an ordinary head. There are no visible abnormalities. The hair that covers it is inoffensive. It isn't, say, a riotous orange or the brassy yellow acquired from a bottle of peroxide. It is merely brown and unlikely to cause unfavorable comment unless one is disturbed by mediocrity. The hair is neatly parted, only slightly skewed near the crown, and the scalp exposed in the part is pink; the hair is clean.

Overall, there is nothing particularly distasteful about the head. But B. Lynn, looking down from her perch in a young tree, believes it is the most loathsome object she has ever contemplated and she prepares to spit on it. As she leans over to take aim her sister, Soozie-Bells, lifts her face to peer up through the leaves of the tree. B. Lynn quickly swallows her ammunition and scrubs her feet against slippery bark, in order to elevate herself more distantly from the face that is even more objectionable than the head. The sisters quietly observe each other and the feelings of animosity are mutual.

Soozie-Bells finally says, *It's time for dinner.*

While there is nothing intrinsically unpleasant about that statement, B. Lynn doesn't like the way it has been said. It has been said with a tone of authority that rankles her and so she replies, "Drop dead." Soozie-Bells shrugs and walks away.

B. Lynn watches as she saunters across the street. It is a superior saunter; it is the walk

of a sister who believes she always has the upper hand because she is six years older. Soozie-Bells' method of walking enrages B. Lynn. She would like to jump down from her tree and twist her fingers around until they snap right off her skinny hands like splintered Popsicle sticks.

Instead, she flings a single mud word. As soon as the word is launched B. Lynn realizes her error, and almost falls off her tree branch trying to grab the darn thing so she can stuff it back into her mouth. Too late: it soars toward its target with the speed and precision of a Nike missile and splats right on the back of her sister's disgusting head.

B. Lynn stops breathing and fervently hopes Soozie-Bells will turn around and throw an equally illegal word back, thus effectively canceling out the one that just escaped from her own mouth. But Soozie-Bells only stands still, and after a silent moment of reflection, squares her shoulders and leaves off sauntering in favor of a stiff-legged march into their house. She is perfectly aware she holds B. Lynn's fate securely in her hands.

Suffering interrogation at the family dinner table confessional, B. Lynn's mother says to her, *WHAT did you call your sister today?*

B. Lynn thinks the consequences of her verbal transgression might be less severe if she spells the word: "A... s..." But as soon as the letters reluctantly crawl out of her mouth, she realizes spelling it sounds the same as saying it—except with a Southern accent.

You called her WHAT?

"An ass! I called her an ASS!" She quickly looks up and there it is: the ass word cantering about in the sacred realm of the dining room, braying and bucking obscenely over the Sunday roast... upsetting the bowls of mashed potatoes and peas.

Her mother recoils and then leaps from her chair. She yanks B. Lynn from the table with a one-arm dangle-and-drag, and vigorously applies the palm of her hand to the part of her daughter's body that has ruined Sunday dinner. She uses a cake of Lifebuoy soap to scrub the word off B. Lynn's tongue—and

B. Lynn is very sorry she called Soozie-Bells an ass, when she could have called her something worse.

Ape Shit

B. Lynn does not particularly like Kathy. They are reluctant companions because their older sisters are friends, and the older sisters are quite often charged with the task of watching over them. Nobody is happy with this arrangement but their parents.

B. Lynn is twelve-years-old going on eight; Kathy is twelve-years-old going on eighteen. There is an aura of foreignness about Kathy. She doesn't live on Prescott Street. Her house is located in the uncharted territory of Elm Avenue where all the games are played by the wrong rules. B. Lynn is surprised they speak the same language.

Although there are few places B. Lynn won't go, Kathy crosses over boundaries into areas that make her uneasy—until Kathy introduces a pursuit that holds her interest: they will learn to smoke.

Hunkered behind B. Lynn's garage, they practice the art of inhalation. As they are coughing, choking and generally enjoying themselves, they notice a suspicious movement in the bushes. Because B. Lynn is twelve-years-old going on eight and Kathy is twelve-years-old going on eighteen, B. Lynn figures Kathy has had more experience investigating suspicious movements in bushes and tells her so.

Kathy scrubs her streaming eyes and nose on the front of her shirt and walks cautiously toward the wagging limbs. Keeping her eyes trained on the bushes, she squats down and dusts her hands through the grass until her right hand latches onto a twig. She employs the twig to poke gingerly in the branches.

Kathy abruptly stands up and claps her hands a couple of times. She squints in the bushes and then saunters back to B. Lynn. "What the heck was in there?" B. Lynn asks.
Just a damned monkey.

***

Five years later, B. Lynn is strolling down a sidewalk minding her own business, taking pleasure that no one else is minding it for her. She is musing about life and boys; the prospect of leaving for college in the fall and more boys.

She is jolted out of her reverie when she feels a disturbance on her back. B. Lynn is squirrel-phobic and she knows every time she takes a walk the chances of having one tumble out of a tree and land on her increase. She has taken many walks, so the risk is great. Panicked, she twists and turns, slaps at her back, and scatters her hands through her hair until she is convinced she is rodent-free.

She continues on her way, anxiously scanning the trees for wildlife, until her back suddenly screams, *SQUIRREL!* She dashes to a fence and scootches her back on the post like a flea-bitten ass. There is a soft thud on the ground; B. Lynn looks down and shrieks. A monkey looks up and shrieks.

Feeling distinctly weasel-ish, she charges down the street with the monkey hot on her heels. The monkey makes a wild leap and clutches her shirt. B. Lynn snags the hideous thing by its tail and flings it down hard on the sidewalk. She jumps up and down on its head—grabs it around the neck and squeezes until its eyes bulge. But she just can't kick that monkey. Nope, she absolutely cannot kick that monkey.

B. Lynn sits down and stares at the monkey. The monkey sits down and stares at her. The monkey doesn't blink and neither does she. B. Lynn remembers the day Kathy saw this monkey in the bushes. She sighs and says, "Guess I'm going to be lugging your monkey ass around for the rest of my life."

The monkey curls his lip and screeches. He pulls a cigarette from behind his big old monkey ear and hands it to her.

Dumbfounded

B. Lynn's mother drags a man dummy out of the garage and into the house. She heaves him into a chair in the living room, thrusts a pipe in his mouth and a newspaper in his hands.

Kneeling in front of him, she unlaces his right shoe and flings it across the room. The laces on the left shoe are snaked in an unforgiving tangle. She picks and pulls but they refuse to give up their knots. Biting her lip, she grabs hold of the shoe and jerks it around until it pops off in her hands. She stuffs his feet into bedroom slippers.

There are paint tears, the color of the house, on the man dummy's glasses. She scrapes at them with her thumbnail and then scrapes at her thumbnail with her front teeth. She spits the paint tears, the color of the house, from her mouth.

Tugging a second chair across the room she angles it, just so, next to the man dummy's chair and teeters a pole lamp between them, hovering her hands until the lamp steadies.

A teen-aged girl dummy is tucked in a bedroom. B. Lynn's mother pounds up the stairs, grabs her up by the ankles and thumps her down the steps. She flips her into the chair next to the man dummy's and clamps a copy of 'Seventeen Magazine' in her hands.

Pausing, thinking, she races to the book shelf and streams her forefinger along the spines of the books until she finds a big one—a book with some heft to it. She snatches the magazine from the teen-aged girl dummy's hands and replaces it with 'War and Peace.'

The hair on the teen-aged girl dummy is twisted tightly into curls, secured with bobby pins and bound with a white kerchief. B. Lynn's mother pokes a bobby pin, sliding from its nest, back into place and then sucks her finger where the unguarded tip of the bobby pin has drawn a hint of blood.

Squinting into corners and under furniture, she locates a little girl dummy and a mutt dummy heaped together beneath the dining room table. She crawls under the table, latches onto the little girl dummy's arm, the mutt dummy's tail, and trundles them into the living room. She molds the little girl dummy into a sitting position in front of the man dummy's chair and crosses her legs. The legs spring apart. She folds them back into place.

The little girl dummy is clenching a cap gun in her fist. B. Lynn's mother grapples with the fist until the gun thuds softly onto the carpet. She bends the little girl dummy's fingers around a miniature baby bottle and arranges a Tiny Tears doll on her lap.

There is a grape jelly birthmark on the little girl dummy's left cheek. With spit-licked fingers B. Lynn's mother scrubs at the purple stain, until nothing is left on the cheek but a hot circular flush.

Turning, she leans over and clasps her hands under the mutt dummy's belly and hoists her into a standing position. She supports the mutt dummy's chest with one hand as she pushes down on her rear-end with the other. She yanks a bedroom slipper off the man dummy's foot, pries open the mutt dummy's jaws and inserts the slipper.

The mutt dummy's long ears are matted with burdock. She rakes her fingers on the clumps until she is startled by a low growl. Quickly pulling back her hand she notices her fingers, sticky from the little girl dummy's grape jelly birthmark, have attracted small tufts of light brown fur. She vigorously rubs her hands together until the fur rolls into skinny worms, easily flicked to the floor.

B. Lynn's mother studies the scene for a moment and then rips the newspaper from the man dummy's hands, adjusting his head so it appears as if he is fondly gazing down at the little girl dummy on the floor.

Walking a short distance across the living room, she stands with her back to the dummies and tries to un-imagine the tableau she has created, so it will be a surprise when she turns to look. Spinning around, she is immediately struck with a great deal of crankiness and not a little disgust: despite her artful maneuverings, B. Lynn's father, Soozie-Bells, B. Lynn and Puddy-Pup still resemble four dingy potatoes, lately retrieved from the root cellar.

The dummies fade into the beige wall behind them, and it occurs to B. Lynn's mother that if they were propped against a different backdrop, bright and fresh, they might come to take on the same qualities. She lets her eyes paint the beige wall yellow. The yellow wall is refreshing, but the dummies are still beige and it's still the same old wall. Turquoise slides over the yellow. Turquoise is daring, but the dummies are still beige and it's still the same old wall. Concentrating, B. Lynn's mother makes her eyes slap up some red plaid wallpaper. In a blink, her affronted eyes shove turquoise back into place.

Rubbing the back of her neck, B. Lynn's mother thinks the dummies might always look beige if she always has to look at them against the same old wall. She decides there is nothing to be done but sell their house and buy another—a house with a new wall, bright and fresh.

She snaps her fingers and the dummies scatter.

The Least You Need to Know

Her mother tells her she'll have a bigger yard to play in when they move to the new house and B. Lynn doesn't think that makes one bit of sense. She doesn't understand why she should drag her Prescott Street friends all the way across town to play in a bigger yard when they already have a whole block to run around in and she tells her mother so. Her mother says she isn't going to be dragging any Prescott Street kids across town to play, and B. Lynn asks her then who the heck is she supposed to play with. Her mother says she will play with the children she meets in the new neighborhood and she can bring her school friends home.

B. Lynn doesn't like children she doesn't know—especially children who are called children—and she doesn't have any school friends, unless the janitor who always pats her on the head counts. She asks her mother if the janitor who always pats her on the head counts. Her mother snaps, *I don't care who they are as long as it isn't your gang of street thugs.*

Her mother informs her when they move to the new house she's going to be summoning her with a bell. B. Lynn has never seen anyone summon someone with a bell except rich people in the movies, and she wonders why her mother has suddenly come to believe she has the skills required of a maid.

She tells her mother she guesses she won't mind too much about having to do all the work around the house and wait on people, as long as she doesn't have to wear a frilly cap. Her mother wants to know what she is talking about and B. Lynn says, "The maid bell."

Her mother says, *What maid bell.*

"The maid bell you're going to use to summon me. I'm not wearing a frilly cap."

I don't know anything about a maid bell. B. Lynn thinks it might go easier on her mother if she just pounded on the walls to summon her, rather than having to study-up on how to use the darned bell and she tells her mother so.

Silent a moment, B. Lynn's mother finally says, *We're going to hang a bell by the back door and I'm going to ring it when it's time for you to come home.* B. Lynn is baffled by this outlandish notion because everyone knows mothers scream up and down the street when they want people to come home. She asks her mother why she needs to use a bell and her mother says, *Because I'm not going to scream up and down the street.*

B. Lynn wants to know how she's supposed to tell when it's her bell ringing and her mother snaps, *You just will.* B. Lynn suggests maybe they could figure out a special ring like Morse code or something, so she'll know for sure when it's her bell. Her mother says she isn't going to talk about it anymore and walks out of the kitchen.

B. Lynn yells, "What KIND of bell?"

Just a BELL for crying out loud.

There isn't a sidewalk at the new house which makes it almost like being in the country, so B. Lynn decides it might be a cow bell—although she's pretty sure there's a law against people keeping them as pets, which is a shame because she personally would love to have her own cow.

It occurs to her if the parents in the new neighborhood call their kids home with cow bells maybe it's because they look like cows. She thinks of fat doughy kids stumping back to their barns at feeding time.

She's never known any doughy kids except Deborah at school who has a metabolical problem, and she's never had a chance to touch her. She wonders if doughy kids are hard or fluffy, and if they play football which would be the best way for them to feel. Blocking a fluffy one might be like sinking into a big marshmallow—in which case she'd have to fight through all their fluff until she reached something solid to push against. If they're hard she's going to make darn sure she doesn't get tackled.

B. Lynn trails after her mother and asks if doughy kids play football. Her mother says, *What are you talking about.*

"Doughy kids. Do they play football."

What doughy kids.

"The kids in the new neighborhood." Her mother asks what makes her think the kids in the new neighborhood are doughy and B. Lynn says, "The cow bell."

What cow bell.

"The one that's going to hang by the back door."

I don't know anything about a cow bell.

B. Lynn thinks about what the new neighbors will have to say when they see her mother fumbling and clanging around not using the bell properly. She thinks about the doughy kids who will know it's her mother who doesn't know the first thing about bells. She stares at her mother and says, "Well when are you going to learn how to use it?"

Learn how to use what?

"The bell that's going to hang by the back door."

For chrissakes just come home when I ring the damned bell—and B. Lynn realizes she knows exactly how to properly ring her mother's bell.

Up to Her Ears

B. Lynn stares at the words scrawled on the inside back wall of her school locker: B. LYNN IS FULL OF SLIT. It appears the author of this statement was in a very big hurry or doesn't know how to spell and although B. Lynn is fairly certain of the intent, she tries substituting other letters in case her interpretation of the message is incorrect: *Spit?* She hasn't been inclined to spit in at least a year. *Skit?* Perhaps someone thinks she is a fine actress. *Snit?* She is known to be easily irritated.

But nothing seems to fit quite as well as the letter 'h.' B. Lynn thinks B. LYNN IS FULL OF SLIT might be a fairly accurate analysis of her personality, and she hopes her new pen pal can keep this information just between the two of them. She takes a final look at her personal greeting—written indelibly in black Magic Marker so generations of eighth-graders will know what she is full of—and quietly closes her locker door.

Navigating her way down the school corridor is a difficult process. Her wretched quivering mess of a thirteen-year-old body—a body that sporadically leaks and sprouts stuff—is attached to legs that won't let her walk like a normal person.

She experiments with various methods of ambulating: scuffing her heels and slouching feels about right—except her hands are flopping at her sides like a couple of dead fish. She tightens her arms and clenches her fists, but the rigid posturing of her arms and hands seems at odds with the casual approach of scuffing and slouching. Straightening her back, she adopts a purposeful stride until she realizes the erection of her spine causes some of her growths to be more noticeable; she quickly hunches over and walks into English class looking like an ape.

Sitting at her desk she tries to make her neck hold her head in a reasonable position.

As the day muddles by it becomes clear that the knowledge of what B. Lynn is full of, has spread through the school like head lice. She is a steel ball in a pinball machine: when she approaches a cluster of kids they thrust her away to send her spinning and ricocheting off other bumpers.

This creates a problem for her eyes. She doesn't want to be caught looking at people who aren't looking at her. She moves through the hallways with her eyes straight ahead and unfocused as she practices appropriate facial expressions.

Standing in the entrance to the cafeteria, perspiring freely, B. Lynn wonders where she is allowed to sit. She looks out the corners of her eyes at her customary table where there is a good deal of whispering and chortling going on, and B. Lynn is certain she hears someone hiss *full of.*

She notices a jumble of clique-less kids who don't seem to be aware of her locker message. However, she still has social standards so she heads for an empty table, tight-lipped and goose-stepping like a soldier in Chairman Mao's army, because her knees have forgotten how to bend.

That evening, B. Lynn is a reluctant participant in a game her father enjoys: Inquisition.

Did you do anything to help your mother today? her father asks.

"Mmmm…"

How was school?

"GOOD!"

Did you pass your math test?

"Uh-huh."

Have you finished your homework?

"Yep."

She holds her father's stare until her eyes get interested in something on the floor. In the weighted silence that follows B. Lynn knows her father knows she is absolutely—unequivocally—full of slit.

Cracked

If she had proper surgical equipment the operation would be going much more smoothly. But with nothing on hand except a pair of fingernail scissors, she is forced to hack away at her right leg like Lizzie Borden with PMS. The scissors slip from B. Lynn's trembling fingers and clatter onto the bathroom floor. The sound ricochets off the tiled walls, tap dances on the mirror over the sink, plays a few stanzas of 'Wipe Out' on the toilet lid, and then assaults her ears where it joins the commotion of her pounding heart. When she is certain all the clattering and heart pounding haven't alerted her parents to the nefarious activities taking place in the bathroom, she resumes chopping and slicing at her leg until the results of her surgery lie scattered across the floor like turquoise confetti. Her left leg is more amenable to the pointing of toes and twisting of ankle required to escape the bondage of her tight turquoise stretch pants, and so she is able to quickly remove the remaining un-hacked portions of her ski clothes.

Head spinning and nausea boiling, she eases into the bathtub of steaming water and watches her right foot and ankle blossom into a large purple eggplant. As she lies soaking and shivering, B. Lynn mulls over the conversation with her mother earlier that morning, looking for loopholes that might be used to blame her injury on something other than herself:

"Jill asked me to go skiing at Emery Park with her and a bunch of some other kids."

No. You've only had one lesson. You'll break your neck.

"It's just a little hill."

You have a math exam tomorrow morning.

"I've already studied."

Then go. But you better pass that exam and you BETTER NOT GET HURT.

The discussion leaves little room for verbal maneuvering. It is loop-less and wrapped up tighter than leftover fish in cellophane. So that her mother will never know that she has gone and done exactly what she was told not to do, B. Lynn decides she has no alternative but to endure the pain of the traitorous ankle until it heals or rots right off her leg.

The next morning, lurching the half-mile through snow to the high school on Main Street, B. Lynn worries about falling in a snow bank. She wonders if anyone would come looking for her, or if she would have to lie there until spring. She thinks about being a member of the Donner Party and eating her mother.

Arriving at school, B. Lynn gazes up at the three flights of stairs she has to climb to get to the exam room. They are the Rocky Mountains: she will press on with fortitude and spirit. She grabs the railing... quicksteps... grunts... drags and pauses. B. Lynn uses this formula to climb the first flight of stairs, and then checks her watch: Grab—quickstep—grunt—drag—pause.

Collapsing into her chair, she is more concerned about the possibility of throwing up all over her desk than she is about the math midterm. She scribbles down random numbers, which is not too unlike the method she uses under normal circumstances.

B. Lynn is sick and tired. She is sick and tired of her ankle; she is sick and tired of math exams; she is sick and tired of herself. In fact, she is so sick and tired of everything she doesn't care if she is grounded for the rest of her miserable life.

Hobbling to the school office, she asks to use the telephone. She calls her mother for a ride home and confesses her lack of skiing judgment.

***

54%... B. Lynn stares hard at her math grade and her mother stares hard at her, the report card lying between them on the table and stinking up the whole kitchen. Her mother taps her fingernails, each tap adding another weight onto B. Lynn's scale of terror.

She suffers a slight convulsion when her mother abruptly stands up, walks to the telephone, and calls the school: *She had a broken ankle when she took her math exam. No, it wasn't in a cast—she was walking all over TOWN on it for crying out loud, with a temperature of a hundred-and-one. Uh huh... yes... thank you.*

Her mother hangs up the telephone, turns to B. Lynn and says, *They're going to change your grade to a passing sixty-five percent.* They look hard at each other, both knowing she has never in her entire life passed anything that involves numbers.

B. Lynn begins planning the breakage of another body part before her final math exam in the spring.

Mistaken Identity

B. Lynn knows two important things about ministers: they have schizophrenic personalities and they tend to flock around dead people. She can't fathom why they're allowed to behave as they do—if she went around broadcasting that God was whispering various instructions in her ear and she was having visions of holy lights—she's pretty sure her mother would bundle her up and dump her at the front door of The Gowanda State Mental Asylum.

Her only conclusion is that the attraction of attending church is similar to that of going to a sideshow at the county fair—except the sideshow costs fifty cents whereas in church you can pay whatever you want. She, herself, enjoys a good sideshow—but until someone proves that proximity with ministers doesn't increase proximity with death she would rather take her chances living as a heathen.

As such, B. Lynn does not appreciate coming home from school to discover a minister standing in the middle of her living room. She especially doesn't like coming home from school to discover a minister standing in the middle of her living room and holding her mother's hand. This is a shocking display, as her mother has often expressed her own distaste for the clergy— although she reserves more rancor for priests and nuns.

She hasn't seen him in years, but B. Lynn recognizes this particular species of minister as being of the First Presbyterian variety; one who is especially troublesome because he has a girl's name and that name belongs to her: he is the Reverend B. Lynne. Before her parents decided they would rather sin than be saved, she had spent many Sunday mornings anxiously scanning his face for a family resemblance.

B. Lynn hopes her mother isn't going to start letting all kinds of riff-raff traipse through the house now that her father isn't living at home to act as a sand bag against her sporadic tornadic behavior. Having read the Ask Heloise column in the newspaper, her mother had acted on Heloise's advice and purged the house of clutter and objects she no longer found useful. Despite B. Lynn's protests that she would like to keep her father, feeling he has great sentimental value, her mother packed him up and tossed him into a motel room on the outskirts of town.

The minister and her mother are not aware B. Lynn is observing them; domestic volatility and the general eighth-grade opinion that she is full of *slit* have encouraged her to train in the art of invisibility. She is very good at it; most of the time she is invisible.

Touring her eyes around their hands she sees they are not romantically entwined, but are rather forming a kind of inside out sandwich: her mother's hand a solitary slice of white bread clamped between the minister's hands that look like two cuts of marbled pork.

Leaning close to her mother's face the minister says, *God will guide you through these troubled waters. All you have to do is listen for Him.*

B. Lynn doesn't believe her mother needs any encouragement to develop more mental health issues so she steps further into the living room and says, "I'm home."

Her mother skitters a look at her and slides her hand out of the cold pork. The minister turns and gazes at B. Lynn with funereal eyes, giving her the understanding that her father must be dead. She yells, "IS MY FATHER DEAD?"

Your father isn't dead for crying out loud, her mother replies. *It's your sister.*

"MY SISTER'S DEAD??"

She's gone.

B. Lynn yells, "My sister's DEAD and GONE?" She throws a wild look at the minister who is studying her like she's some kind of odd fungus that has suddenly sprouted on the living room carpet.

Her mother says, *She ran away from home for God's sake.* B. Lynn thinks Soozie-Bells should have run away for her own sake—not God's sake—and she can't figure what the heck a minister has to do with anyone's sake—unless he was mentally rehabilitated and now he's a cop.

B. Lynn has always been under the impression when a person was eighteen they were allowed to run away from home and Soozie-Bells is eighteen. She says, "Soozie-Bells eighteen." *Don't tell me how old your sister is,* her mother snaps. *I was there when she was born.*

If it's still illegal to run away from home when a person gets to be that old, B. Lynn decides it doesn't make sense for her to hang around six more years waiting for her eighteenth birthday. She might just as well skedaddle now, while she's only twelve and can still run fast.

The Reverend B. Lynne gazes mournfully at her mother and says, *I'll be in touch.* As he moves toward the door, he pauses by B. Lynn and hovers his pork hand over her head with the intention of patting—but B. Lynn, weak with terror that she is about to be blessed, stumbles backward leaving his hand in the embarrassing situation of finding itself hanging in the air with nothing to do. The Reverend B. Lynne arcs his hand to the top of his own head, rakes it through his imaginary hair, and then steps carefully out the door.

B. Lynn stares at her mother across the empty air of the living room and her mother stares at her, until all the staring is ricocheting off the walls. Her mother eventually shrugs and says, *I needed someone to talk to.* Although B. Lynn is glad her mother didn't want to talk to her—she's had plenty of talking to from her mother—she still can't figure why she would choose a minister as her new best friend, an association that could quickly turn deadly and land her prematurely in hell.

A niggling thought bores into B. Lynn's brain: she slams out the front door and chases the Reverend B. Lynne's car down the driveway. He brakes harshly and thrusts his head out his window. Panting, B. Lynn yells, "Are you my FATHER?"

The Reverend B. Lynne frowns and says, *Of course not dear, I'm a Protestant.*

Say Uncle

He was a tobacco-chewing, hard-drinking, slow-moving, rough-and-tumble man, with a sweet smile and a glass eyeball and he was known as Big Bart. B. Lynn called him Uncle Bart, and he called her Kid.

B. Lynn's mother worshipped the red Arkansas dirt Big Bart walked on. He was her favorite older brother and knew she was his favorite younger sister because she was the recipient of all his brotherly love: he teased and tormented her to distraction.

She regaled her daughters with tales of her childhood and told them stories that provided evidence of Big Bart's affection. They listened with a delicious mixture of horror and fascination, and B. Lynn wished she had a brother.

Her mother waxed nostalgic of the times Big Bart held her captive under a bed, banging at her fingers with a stick when she tried to crawl out, all the while demanding, *SAY UNCLE.* She would sooner be beaten to death with the stick than say *Uncle*. As a result, she spent a great deal of time trapped beneath the bed, building dust castles and idly plunking out tunes on the bedsprings with her finger.

She demonstrated on her writhing and shrieking daughters the way he used to wrestle her to the ground and pin her there as he slowly, very slowly, released a string of saliva from his mouth. He let it dangle like a pendulum just inches away from her shocked eyes before he slurped it back up and said, *Say UNCLE.* But B. Lynn's mother never would.

***

Face down, B. Lynn plows through the icy water of Cherokee Lake. She has been skiing on her face for at least an

92

hour. Her cheeks are raw and her arms feel like two rubber bands yanked to the point of snapping. She hopes by the time her feet figure out how to get to where her face is, her arms won't be so stretched out that her hands hang down below her knees.

She unclenches her grip on the tow rope and bobs around while Aunt Frieda gathers it into the boat and then hurls it back into the water. When B. Lynn grabs the rope she yells, *Girl, you are a glutton for punishment.* Uncle Bart guns the boat forward with enough speed to fling B. Lynn to the moon; she pulls herself up and out of the water and triumphantly wobbles on two skis.

He allows her about five minutes to become proficient at wobbling before he begins steering the boat in circles, creating waves so high that B. Lynn believes she might do better with a surfboard. As she flounders through water washing over her skis, she hears Uncle Bart yell those thrilling words: *SAY UNCLE.* She shakes her head. No, she will not say *Uncle.*

Straightening the tiller, he gestures with his arm, encouraging her to ski out to the side of the boat where the water is glassy and smooth. B. Lynn skis left and he turns right. She swings wide and wild, moving so fast she feels like a tetherball that has just been smacked by a thousand-pound gorilla. Uncle Bart's voice spirals back in a rush of wind: *Say UNCLE.* She tightens her lips so her mouth can't smile, and shakes her head. He doesn't drive the boat reasonably until he is satisfied that she won't say *Uncle* and, should the occasion arise, she could ski through a tsunami.

For the remainder of the weekend, B. Lynn wanders around in a haze of glory: Uncle Bart tried to kill her and she didn't say *Uncle.*

On the ride home, wedged between Uncle Bart and Aunt Frieda in the front seat of their pickup truck, B. Lynn wonders if it's possible that she will get drunk on her aunt and uncle's whiskey and beer-breath fumes.

Aunt Frieda slouches against her—she is uncomfortably close—and slurs, *Sing a song. Your Uncle Bart's fallin' asleep.*

B. Lynn ratchets her head left to look at him. His eyes droop once, twice, and his shoulders sag to the level of the steering wheel. Grabbing onto the first song that enters her head, she belts out a hectic rendition of 'Found a Peanut.' Uncle Bart jerks up straight and when she finishes he says, *That was a mighty purty song, Kid.*

She lapses into silence, worrying about who's going to sing if she gets knocked cold on the secondhand whiskey and beer fug. Aunt Frieda gives her a jab with her elbow and mumbles, *Keep singin', he's fallin' asleep agin.* B. Lynn launches into 'Ninety-nine Bottles of Beer on the Wall,' shouting out the song as if her life depended on it, and wishing the double yellow lines on the road were passing to the left instead of slicing under the middle of the truck. Counting backward from ninety-nine is mentally fatiguing, so when she finishes yelling about too many bottles of beer she switches to 'Wooly Bully,' an easy song because no one can understand the words, and thus requires little concentration to perform a competent version of it: "**Dah**-da-dah-**dah**-da-wooly-bully! Wooly bully."

B. Lynn bounces in her seat, she's really feeling the music now and getting to the best stanza: "Dah-**dah**-da-**dah**-dah-**dah**—"when Uncle Bart decides the asshole in the car in front of them is driving dangerously close to the front of his truck. He veers into the passing lane and B. Lynn's eyes lock on the approaching cement truck that's getting larger by the second. She screams, "Uncle! For cripessakes–UNCLE!"

Checking Regrets Only

She laughs. It is a short laugh—really more like a bark. The short barking laugh isn't a reaction to something funny, but rather an outburst caused by incredulity. She thinks her mother has just said: *Theresa-Maria is deaf,* and that is a horrid notion and too ridiculous. B. Lynn doesn't believe a thirteen-year-old girl she has been friends with her entire life would suddenly be deaf because things like that don't happen to people she knows. People she knows don't just wake up one morning with their ears not working properly.

She doesn't understand why her mother has flown all the way from Fair Field, New York to Little Rock, Arkansas to bother her and talk nonsense in the airport parking lot and ruin the rest of her summer vacation with her aunts and uncles. Her mother is looking at her like SHE'S the one who's out of her mind and then she repeats what she just said, and what she just said was not *Theresa-Maria is deaf.* What she just said was: *Theresa-Maria is DEAD.*

B. Lynn doesn't respond to this piece of information because she is preoccupied with the pavement tilting and sliding around under her feet. She stomps her foot down hard to make the pavement behave and notices an ant staggering past her foot. It's unusual to see an ant wandering around out in the middle of an airport parking lot and she feels sorry. A parking lot is a lousy place for an ant— especially when there are perfectly nice fields of hay or some such stuff nearby that would probably be much more ant friendly than an asphalt dessert—although it would be a really long ant walk across the parking lot because it doesn't have a single tuft of grass and she's pretty sure ants have to suck on grass to get a drink of water.

She wonders if it is lost or if it has friends that are also enduring wretched thirsty lives without grass in a parking lot that is hotter than the eternal fires of damnation burning up through her sneakers all the way to her head and causing her face and back and sides to shiver from sweat. It seems impossible that it can stand on its tiny ant feet without getting fried.

Last year in seventh grade her social studies teacher had an Exotic Food Day at school and he brought rattlesnake meat, fried grasshoppers and chocolate covered ants for the class to sample. She didn't eat any of the snake even though it was skinned and cut up into pieces so it didn't look snake-ish— just pink chunks of flesh. The fried grasshoppers were ok—small bits of grease with a little crunch. But the chocolate covered ants were delicious and she ate a lot of those. They tasted like the chocolate covered raisins in the bridge mix her mother sets out when company comes.

But the thought of eating chocolate covered ants right now in a sizzling parking lot with oozing pockets of dark chocolate tar makes her feel like she might gag and she does gag. She watches the ant's progress until it disappears into a crack. So that's where it lives—it lives in a damned hole in the ground.

B. Lynn looks up so swiftly at the sky her neck bones crack and she is surprised the sun is still shining—not a cloud in sight. An airplane roars over, casting a brief shadow and flying so low it looks as if it just might graze the top of her head. Her mother's words are whining in her head like a mosquito in the dead of night, B. Lynn claps her hands over her ears but her mother's voice bleeds through her fingers.

A few summers ago she smacked Theresa-Maria on the head—hard enough to knock her glasses cockeyed—and Theresa-Maria ran into her house crying. When she came back outside she said she had to take an aspirin because the smacking on her head made it ache and B. Lynn wishes now that she hadn't done that. She hopes the smacking wasn't the beginning of the end for Theresa-Maria because didn't her mother just say her brain swelled and that's why she died?

B. Lynn's eyes swim down from the sky to her mother— her neck feels stiff and that's a symptom of what Theresa-Maria had—*spinal meningitis*—and it is dammit-all hard to breathe in a hot parking lot with tar and airplane fumes and car exhaust.

Her mother's cigarette smoke yellows the air and she says, *Jesus called Theresa-Maria home to heaven*— and that's just about the funniest thing B. Lynn's heard all day because she can't remember the last time her mother went to church.

But Theresa-Maria loved going to church. She had a picture in her bedroom of Jesus hanging on a cross with blood dripping—B. Lynn doesn't know how she slept with a grisly picture like that in her bedroom but Theresa-Maria was crazy about Jesus—she was just nuts over him. She also had a cross that she had made with partially burned wooden matchsticks hanging over her bed—she won a prize in Sunday school for making the thing. And she wore a picture of Jesus around her neck. It was called a scapula or something like that and B. Lynn used to make fun of her and call it a SCABula. She also used to tell Theresa-Maria to go home and wash the dirt off her face on those Wednesdays when she had ashes smeared on her forehead and she wishes now that she hadn't said those things.

Then B. Lynn's mother solemnly says, *Jesus loves Theresa-Maria very much so he invited her to live with him* and B. Lynn busts out laughing. She shouldn't be laughing—she doesn't know why she is laughing. But she does know an invitation from Jesus is something she can live without. And she sure as hell isn't going to get too chummy with him.

Souvenir

The man Aunt Frieda calls Buddy—her brother—nods and says, *Go ahead Sweetheart I want you to pick something out in my house that you can take home to remember us by. Anything you want.* B. Lynn gazes at him, she doesn't want to take any of his stuff but he's proud and happy to have it to offer and that makes her sad and that makes him dear.

His fingernails, the topography and hue of which are like tight-lipped oysters, lead his hand in a sweep around the room. *Anything you want,* he says.

Tell him you want them andirons—they was supposed to be mine. B. Lynn leans away from Aunt Frieda telling her to take the andirons—they were supposed to be hers—because Aunt Frieda has pushed her lips in closely uncomfortable proximity to B. Lynn's left ear. The lips are scaling coral lipstick that trails beyond the landscape of her mouth—and issuing from that mouth is a combustible cloud of Schlitz and gin. Aunt Frieda nudges nearer, shifting B. Lynn onto a couch spring sawing through clots of defeated foam cushioning.

B. Lynn studies the linoleum floor shaded yellow—maybe tan—maybe no color at all—and edges her toe into a crack that angles haphazardly across the room. Her toe takes satisfaction in worming back and forth in the grit of grime serving as grout.

Five pairs of lemur-like eyes will her to raise her head and look at them and so she does. The eyes belong to a scratchy-looking gaggle of kids clustered just outside the door, a screen door bereft of screen propped open to let in more air. B. Lynn can only figure the need to hold open a door that's still open when it's closed is because these folks know to take advantage of any scrap of comfort that comes their way—and eliminating the two-inch perimeter of door frame might free more breeze than she knows.

One kid scuffs in the dirt by the door and says, *Daddy said pick something we don't care what. You can have it.* B. Lynn can't tell if he's eager for her to find the perfect thing to take home to remember him by—or if he'd appreciate it if she'd hurry up and get gone out of his house so there's room for him and his brothers and sisters to come back inside. If the latter is the case, she would very much like to accommodate him. She worries he might be thinking she's going to take the couch home to remember him by—which she would never do because the only other provision for sitting is an uneasy aluminum lawn chair of haggard orange and white webbing— and the man Aunt Frieda calls Buddy is taking up all the room in that for himself.

B. Lynn sags under the awful weight of the task set before her. A cuckoo clock lists against a hubcap, the bird stunned and speechless; the pull chains and leaded acorn weights sprawl obscenely across the floor. She speculates about how Aunt Frieda would like that—if she chose a hubcap instead of the andirons that were supposed to be hers.

Her attention snags on a pink Princess telephone nesting in newspapers. The cord is intimately engaged with a tangle of Christmas lights spilling from a box and the rotary dial is smudged black. B. Lynn believes it would make a fine toy for the little girl pair of eyes and she speculates about how Aunt Frieda would like that—if she walked right over to the Princess phone and handed it to the little girl.

A badminton racket, its round face open-mouthed and gap-toothed lies shocked beneath a chunk of motor—or maybe an engine. It occurs to her that she has spent twelve years on earth without knowing if there's a difference between the two. She tries to remember if the story 'The Little Engine That Could' contains any clues about the matter.

It's a subject she'd like to discuss with Uncle Bart—but upon their arrival in this scabby south-western wedge of Indiana, Uncle Bart announced he didn't expect he was inclined to hang around reunion-izing with Aunt Frieda's family—they're no more than shirt-tails to him anyway and filthy ones to boot. Despite B. Lynn's objections to being left behind to deal with his dirty shirt-tails—and Aunt Frieda—on her own, Uncle Bart said, "Sorry Kid, I've got to go water my hole." He careened his pickup truck back down the dirt road in search of a tavern, leaving B. Lynn's mouth dusty with desertion.

She doesn't know what a carburetor looks like but decides that's what the piece of motor—maybe an engine—is going to be because it's a fun word to roll around in her head. Moving her lips around the letters she eases carburetor quietly from her mouth and she's satisfied that that's exactly the word she wants.

What'd you just say? Aunt Frieda asks.

B. Lynn swallows the carburetor and says, "What—what, specifically, are andirons?"

Pickled in the Middle of the Night

Once a month.
Twice a month.

5:00 p.m.

Ice trays clatter.
Stemmed glasses clink.
Parents love martinis.
With drowned olives.

6:00 p.m.

"Time for dinner?"
No—not yet.

No appetite, anyway.
Anyway, who cares.

7:00 p.m.

"Ready to eat?"
I said no.
"Dad should eat."
He will eat.
"But his diabetes."
He is fine.

Retreat to bedroom.
Carefully close door.

8:00 p.m.

Ice trays crash.
Uncomfortable topics discussed.
Talking personal stuff.

10:00 p.m.

"Dad should eat."
Don't tell us.

                Back to bedroom.
                Turn on music.
                Janis, Jimi, Melanie.

12:00 a.m.

Messy words, slurred.
Belligerent voices escalate.
He says this.
She yells that.

                Turn off music.
                Hears her name.
                She's the problem.
                So they say.

1:30 a.m.

Doors slam closed.
He stumbles twice.
Curses under breath.

1:45 a.m.

Silence, then snoring.

> Dad didn't eat.
> He should have.

2:00 a.m.

> Check the house.
> Lights left on.
> Cigarette left smoldering.
> Air is thick.
> Rooms are cold.
> Let dog out.
> Wait for dog.
> Kiss dog goodnight.
> Share a nuzzle.

7:00 a.m.

Oh—good morning.
"Sure it is."
Did you study?
"Yes, of course."
 Finish your homework?
 "Yes, of course."
Take lunch money.
"I've got it."
See you later.
"Yes, of course."

> Parents don't remember.
> B. Lynn does.

Fast Track

She hadn't planned on kissing the drummer. She hadn't even known there was going to be a band at the party, so it wasn't as if she accepted the date with the popular boy just so she could get at the drummer and kiss him. And she certainly hadn't expected a few kisses would cause such a big stinking uproar. As a matter of fact, the popular boy could have shown her a little consideration. He could have given her a clue that she was sending herself into social purgatory, instead of just standing there watching her engage in kissing the drummer.

Running surveillance on him since fifth grade, B. Lynn is alternately repulsed and fascinated by the drummer's pocked skin, tangled hair and apparent disregard for bathing. He evokes in her feelings similar to that of watching maggots squirm on a garbage can, and yet she is drawn to him. His filthy disreputableness gives him an aura of a little dangerousness, and B. Lynn has a weakness for a little dangerousness.

So kissing the drummer was really just to test her grit; a means of determining her fortitude. Lying on her bed, she stares at the ceiling and mentally draws a scientific outline of her experiment:

A. Reasons for Kissing the Drummer
    1. He presented himself for kissing
    2. It was her first and maybe only opportunity
    3. She wanted to know if she had the stomach for it
B. Results of Kissing the Drummer
    1. All the popular kids think her behavior was appalling
    2. Her date found her actions offensive
    3. She didn't gag or throw up

C. Conclusions
  1. Best not to kiss one boy when you are on a date with another
  2. She will never be popular
  3. She might run another experiment on the drummer's lips

  B. Lynn decides the best way to handle the whole ugly mess of her appalling behavior is to take to her bed and refuse to eat. Not only does being skinny make everything better, this plan has the potential of accomplishing two things: 1.) If and when she returns to school, her frail and weakened condition might garner some sympathy. Maybe the popular boy will believe she was as much a victim of her indiscretion as he was. Perhaps he will think, *Ah, she was unwell. That explains her appalling behavior.* 2.) She will die of starvation.

  She is measuring the diameter of her wrist with her thumb and index finger to see if it has lost any weight, when her mother slams into her bedroom and stares at her. Folding her arms and leaning her left hip against the door frame, she needles her eyes at B. Lynn and lets her silent staring freeze the air.

  When the room is finally cold as a morgue, she says, *Get up out of that bed and eat something.*

  B. Lynn rolls her head back and forth on her pillow and says, "Can't. Too sick."

  What's wrong with you?

  "Nothing. I'm just sick." B. Lynn whispers. She hasn't told her mother she went and kissed a toad when she had the prince because she doesn't believe her mother is the kind of person who would take her disgracefulness lightly.

  Her useless friends do. Her useless friends think her appalling behavior is the funniest thing they've ever heard. Rather than giving her a kindly shoulder to lean on, all they do is scream like hyenas over a fresh carcass and say, *Oh my God I can't believe you did that.*

B. Lynn decides she does not particularly like her friends. She has long suspected them of treachery and she's pretty sure that given the opportunity to hang around with the popular kids, they would desert her as quickly as rats on a sinking ship. She is nothing more to them than an extra body to fill out the numbers at their school lunch table so it will look like they have their own clique.

One of her friends isn't even polite about her ambition to elevate herself into the popular kid's stratosphere—she talks to B. Lynn about it all the time. She acts like B. Lynn is just some old shoe that she might decide to throw in the trash. Also, she's always casually throwing around the popular kids' names as if she has had actual conversations with them.

Her other friend, Constant-Jane, is like hanging around with a loaded gun because you never know when she's going to do something embarrassing. B. Lynn looks like a fool for even associating with her. She sighs and wishes she had at least one decent friend and a peanut butter sandwich.

Her head beginning to feel like a washing machine in the spin cycle, she palpates her stomach to see if it has gotten thin enough to deserve a small taste of something. She is disappointed with the results.

Twisting in her bed sheets and humming Simon and Garfunkel's, 'I Am a Rock,' B. Lynn realizes starving to death is a long, lonely and tedious business. She closes her eyes and thinks about kissing the drummer. She decides it was worth it.

The Eleventh Hour

Smelly Belly found the report card and gave it to his sister Little Toot who gave it to their mother who handed it over to B. Lynn's mother who is shaking it in B. Lynn's face: *Where did this come from?* B. Lynn shoots a venomous look at her mother because her mother knows very well where it came from.

"School."

Where else. B. Lynn's stomach uneasily digests this question.

Where ELSE?

"Our mailbox."

Was it addressed to you?

"Mmm..."

What?

"No!"

What did you do with it after you stole it from the mailbox?

"Do with what?"

Your damned report card!

"I threw it under Smelly Belly's and Little Toot's porch."

I can't hear you.

"I THREW IT UNDER SMELLY BELLY'S AND LITTLE TOOT'S PORCH!"

Why would you do that? B. Lynn thinks her mother might do well to go back to school herself and take a course in logic, because the answer to that question is perfectly obvious: she did that because she thought it might be a good idea to keep her report card information private. And if she had known Smelly Belly and Little Toot were going to suddenly develop an ethical streak she would have thrown it under someone else's porch.

You're failing four subjects... you're failing FOUR SUBJECTS?? B. Lynn is not inclined to confirm that question because she is fairly certain her mother knows how to read, and her dismal grades are slashed clearly in red ink: Eighth Grade Math 58%. Eighth Grade Science 60%. Eighth Grade Social Studies 60%. Eighth Grade English 64%.

B. Lynn doesn't have an opinion about her marks in social studies, science and math, but she thinks her grade in English is offensive and her English teacher is a hateful cow— ruining a perfectly nice subject with diagraming sentences which is too much like trying to figure out math problems.

All the comments say you aren't working up to your abilities—LOOK at this. B. Lynn's mother thrusts the report card under her nose for easy reading. *Why aren't you working up to your abilities?* B. Lynn is silent. She isn't likely to tell her mother she doesn't know how to work up to her abilities because she doesn't know what they are. She doesn't even remember taking a class on abilities and wonders if it was part of Religious Education.

B. Lynn's parents take matters in hand and devise a Plan for Academic Success. She is confined to her bedroom and given a quiz every night:

Did you finish your homework?

"Yes!"

Have you studied?

"Yes!" They believe her affirmative answers because stealing mail doesn't automatically qualify her as a liar.

B. Lynn appreciates her parents' Plan for Academic Success because it gives her the privacy to pursue her preferred studies. Science is cast aside for Jane Austen. Her social studies book suffocates under the weight of Tolstoy. Math worksheets are scattered onto the floor to make room for

Charlotte Bronte. A workbook for diagraming sentences squirms beneath Fitzgerald and Salinger.

When failing reports cards continue to arrive with regularity, B. Lynn's parents are confounded that their involvement in her education hasn't helped her achieve any abilities. They aren't aware, when B. Lynn is secluded in her bedroom, she is mainlining words from the pages of novels. They don't realize their daughter is a junkie struggling with a fiction addiction.

Eventually, B. Lynn discovers with a few hours of intensive study before tests she is able to slide the red grades up to precarious blue grades—although her teachers persist in fussing about her abilities. She employs the Do Nothing/Study Like Hell method for the next few years and manages to slip to the next grade levels.

In the final semester of her senior year in high school, B. Lynn's second-to-last report card arrives. Her mother yells, *You're failing Phys. Ed.? How does anyone FAIL GYM for chrissakes?* B. Lynn knows exactly how anyone can fail gym: they can fail gym by not attending.

Well. I hope you know you can't graduate without it.

B. Lynn stares at her mother and says, "It's a REQUIRED SUBJECT??"—and wonders how the heck a person is supposed to cram for GYM.

There are limited options; there is nothing to do but grovel for leniency from the Gym Nazi—a quasi-woman she has happily antagonized for the last three years.

And so, every morning, in the early hours before the school day begins, grunts and thumps from her terror-driven squat-thrusts echo around the empty gymnasium. She races back to the gym during her study hall periods and performs jumping jacks fueled by panic-induced adrenalin. While her classmates are enjoying their bologna sandwiches and chocolate milk, B.

Lynn lunches on the metallic taste of fear as she sweats through endless sit-ups.

The Gym Nazi grudgingly gives her a final grade of 69% and she teeters past failing grades in her other classes. B. Lynn graduates from high school to the overwhelming relief of her parents, exhausted from the grueling task of implementing their Plan for Academic Success.

She goes to a college that accepts students of inferior quality and resolves to work very hard on the subject of abilities—as soon as she figures out what they are. So as to not to waste time while waiting for enlightenment, she finishes reading 'War and Peace.' When her abilities continue to keep themselves a secret she explores 'Crime and Punishment'—although she already knows plenty about that subject.

Conversation Piece

B. Lynn flicks a look at the boy standing beside her and then looks back down at her feet. She doesn't have a single conversational amenity at her disposal. Her head is as empty as a jack-o-lantern without a candle, except for the few words she has already used: *How are you—Yep—Uh-huh—Good—Okay—Really—Wow.* So that they might sound new and fresh, she mentally experiments with fluffing and decorating them: *How ARE you—Oh my gosh, yes—Great-You betcha—Zounds.*

She slips another glance at the boy standing beside her and tries not to make eye contact. If she makes eye contact he will expect her to say something or he might say something and then she will have to say something in return, and she doesn't own one useful word. But his eyeballs are right there looking at her and he says something so B. Lynn says, "Oh."

The air is sparkling with witticisms and repartee, and other people at the party are acting as if they're having a marvelous time. Other people at the party have plenty of things to talk about—they're frothing at their mouths with plenty of things to talk about—and B. Lynn wonders at their resourcefulness and carefree attitudes.

Then the boy standing beside her says something again so B. Lynn grabs one of her plumped-up declarations and offers it to him, "You betcha!" She clears her throat and smiles a smile that looks more like a grimace. She sighs and tries to look interesting.

Some people stroll over and join B. Lynn and the boy standing beside her. They provide some new conversation fodder so she throws in a tentative remark, but her timing is off: a louder and more determined girl speaks at the same time, so B. Lynn's words drown and she doesn't get any credit for having said something.

It occurs to her that if she animates her face it might look as though she's involved in all the fun. She uses the following techniques as evidence that she is socially engaged:

WISDOM—raise eyebrows and nod head
SHOCK—widen eyes and clamp hand over mouth
DISGUST—wrinkle nose and pull down mouth
DISBELIEF—roll eyes
WHO THE HECK KNOWS—shrug shoulders
AMUSEMENT—open mouth, throw-back head
OF COURSE—slap palm on forehead
SYMPATHY—blink eyes rapidly

B. Lynn continues this method of mute communication until she realizes everyone is looking at her like she's spastic.

More people join them and they form a circle. B. Lynn is edged aside and finds herself standing alone outside the circle; she is stranded in teen-age No Man's Land and the circle is closed up tighter than a hangman's noose. It is a situation that sends her directly into crisis mode. Swaying back and forth she hums an old advertising jingle—*School bells ring and children sing we're off to Robert Hall again! Mother knows for better clothes we're off to Robert*—and gazes at the back of the boy who used to be standing beside her.

The circle begins breaking apart, one couple at a time. They drift into shadows and engage their lips in kissing. B. Lynn feels like an old scuffed suitcase forgotten at the bus station, until the boy standing in front of her suddenly remembers he has brought a pair of lips to the party. He turns around and indicates that he would also like to find some shadows.

This boy is stringy and pale, his eyes small and weasel-ish. He has the overall appearance of something that lives underground. There is a ripe pimple on his left nostril that looks as if it's ready to explode and it makes B. Lynn nervous. But she shrugs and lets him lead her into a shadow. At least her mouth will be useful for something.

1969

It wasn't a tearful farewell. It was clean and easy: they slid neatly away from each other like magnets with incompatible polarizations. There was a lot of sighing done that might have been interpreted as regret, but this was the slow and heavy release of breath that comes after an onerous chore has been gotten through—and B. Lynn and her parents have thoroughly gotten through with each other.

Standing on the sidewalk, B. Lynn impatiently waves the family car away from the curb. She watches her parents fade into dusk, watches until the taillights on her mother's Bonneville blur and smear red in traffic.

So that was that and there she is: in not much of a city to attend not much of a community college. The only thing she knows about the city is the name of the street she's standing on; the only thing she knows about the college is she liked the name when her father told her to *pick one*. And the only person she knows is herself–and she doesn't know herself all that well.

She has arrived a week early for classes—she couldn't arrive early enough—but she doesn't find the prospect of living alone in an empty building in an unknown city the least bit anxious-making: for the past six years her brain had received numerous injections of Novocain.

Feeling the weight of the three story brick building hovering behind her, B. Lynn turns and gives it her regard. Although the interior has been disemboweled and then haphazardly rearranged into six apartments for student housing, the exterior still wears the worn clothing of an old furniture factory.

Crossing the narrow strip of beat-down dirt and clumps of struggling grass, she idly runs her finger along the bricks; rusty red crumbs sprinkle down and color her feet. She thinks of a building built of crumbs and imagines it sifting down on her head, piling up around her until it clogs her mouth and nose; ears and eyes. The notion doesn't particularly concern her.

Turning back to the sidewalk she peers through the growing darkness at her new neighborhood. Having grown-up in Fair Field, NY, she doesn't know much about slums—but she's pretty sure she's smack in the middle of one right now. She thinks living in a slum might be interesting. She thinks living in a slum might be a good place to get comfortable.

A streetlight snaps on and then quivers to stay that way. B. Lynn would just as soon not catch its quivers; she pushes through the groaning door of the apartment building and hesitates—just for a moment—before stepping into the entryway.

***

'The Endless Summer is cockeyed.' Teetering on a chair in her assigned bedroom—there are two others to accommodate three more people, bedrooms she hasn't gone into in case her new roommates have a sneaky way of knowing she was snooping around—B. Lynn carefully peels the tape away from the wall and adjusts the poster until it is perfectly aligned with 'Up The Establishment.'

She hops off the chair and squints at the wall. 'Up The Establishment' suddenly breaks free of its bottom bondage and rolls up like a mutinous window shade. It is having a difficult time breaking its old habit. Her father had found this poster particularly offensive, so it has spent the past year living as a tight tube in the back of her bedroom closet. Now that she is no longer living in Fair Field, New York, B. Lynn plans on being particularly offensive all the time.

Kneeling on the floor, she pulls her best friends out of a box and gently places them alphabetically under the stand for her record player: Jefferson Airplane, Jimi Hendrix, Led Zeppelin, The Beatles. She sits back on her heels and contemplates the arrangement. The Beatles makes her uncomfortable placed, as it is, after Led Zeppelin. She wonders if all the bands that begin with 'The' should be place together in a subcategory and then alphabetized according to the second word in their names—except then she would always have to read 'The' before getting to the actual title.

It occurs to her that people are alphabetized by their last names so maybe her records should be, as well: Company, Holding the and Brother Big? Rascals, Young The? Her thoughts get tangled in the dilemma. Sighing, she shoves the problem into the inaccessible portion of her brain that also stores arithmetic.

There is little to put in the dresser drawers because she would rather root around in a trash can for her clothes than go shopping with her mother. She hasn't yet figured out what kind of person she wants to be so her box of clothes contains a combative assortment of apparel: sweater sets and pantyhose quarrel with jeans more hole than cloth; an army fatigue jacket and scuffed leather boots tussle with a duffle coat and penny loafers. She stares at the pantyhose and then yanks them out of the box and stuffs them into the wastepaper basket.

When all the cardboard boxes yawn empty, she kicks them into a corner—and when she is sure she is where she is and that isn't at home, she curls, snail-like, on her bed and thinks about nothing.

Bliss

So they stood on a street corner in Depew—
Depew for chrissakes—three hours thumbs stuck out
wanting to get going—not really caring—
nobody was waiting at the end of the road
in the beginning of summer
they had all the time in the world.
They experimented with pronouncing Depew
in various ways until a beat-up car
packed full of Indian women—
you could say Indian then—picked them up.
The Indians were having a good old time
a day off the reservation
some money in their pocketbooks.
Franny O'Brien and B. Lynn smooshed
between great mounds of rollicking womanly flesh
that quivered and shook every time
another wave of hilarity rolled through them—
who knows what they were laughing about
but they were having a wonderful day
and Franny O'Brien and B. Lynn were too.
The Indians bought them breakfast
and gave them a five-dollar bill worn out with saving—
Franny O'Brien and B. Lynn protesting and protesting
worried they had more dollars stuffed in their pockets
than the Indians had seen in a year.
The giving made the Indians feel good—
Franny O'Brien and B. Lynn feel bad—
and the next thing they knew
the Indians were pulling them
into their huge marshmallow bosoms

of Cashmere Bouquet and sweat
they were still laughing—
Franny O'Brien and B. Lynn were too—
who knows about what—
and the Indians were waving and yelling
be careful
as Franny O'Brien and B. Lynn
walked down the side of the road
dirt and grit warm on their bare feet
singing 'Me and Bobby McGee'
taking turns reading Kerouac out loud
getting nowhere fast
uh-huh
nobody was waiting at the end of the road
in the beginning of summer
they had all the time in the world.

No Shit

Franny O'Brien didn't want his shit and neither did B. Lynn but here they are looking at it anyway because the flipped-out guy with scrambled hair tossed the mangy cloth sack into their room onto the bed at the boarding house and said, *Hang on to my shit for me will ya.* Franny O'Brien had told him they didn't want his shit in their room but the flipped-out guy said, *Just hang on to it for me will ya* and then he left.

B. Lynn thinks Franny O'Brien should open it up see what's in it but Franny O'Brien says, *I'm not touching that filthy thing what if his dirty underpants are in there.*

"Why would you think that," B. Lynn says.

I don't know maybe he can't find his mother.

"Well if he thinks we're going to wash his dirty underpants he's out of his freaking mind," B. Lynn says. "What do you suppose this place is named after?"

What are you talking about.

"This place—this Iroquois Rooming House place—do you think it was named after an Indian or beer or what."

How would I know it could have been named after Mr. Goddam Fucking Iroquois for all I know, says Franny O'Brien. *Doesn't it smell like pig pee in here? It smells like pig pee in here.*

"What do you know about pig pee."

Plenty.

"I don't think so. I don't think you know the first thing about it."

Have you ever smelled it?

"No. I haven't."

Well I'm telling you this room smells exactly like the urine of a pig.

"So how do you smell it then."

Through my nose for chrissakes.

"No—do you get down on your hands and knees and sniff around near where it's peeing? Ha! Is that what you do? Is that how you know so much about it?"

They spread it around on fields. My God.

"That's disgusting why would somebody do that."

Franny O'Brien says, *I'm through with this conversation* so B. Lynn figures she is too.

"Hey. Where's our bathroom." B. Lynn asks.

Under the bed where do you think.

"Seriously—where's the bathroom."

Down the hall.

"Down the… Sweet Jesus it's a commune bathroom isn't it you know I hate that. Everybody in this whole Mr. Goddam Fucking Iroquois place is going to be using our toilet aren't they. God I hate that. When you paid the lady to stay here you didn't think to specifically ask for a private bathroom did you."

Sure I specifically asked—right after I specifically asked for a room with a view. Then I told her we would like room service and chocolates on our pillows, thank you very much. Good grief what did you expect—besides it's a semi-private the people on the second floor get their own.

"So only about twenty other people are going to be messing around in our bathroom that's a relief. Maybe we can round everybody up and sing 'Kumbaya' together in the bathtub. And somebody could accompany us on the guitar while they're sitting on the toilet. There's probably more than one asshole staying here who can pluck-out a little tune—there's probably plenty of assholes around here that think they're frigging Jimi Hendrix."

Well I'm going to go use it.

"Well I'm coming with you."

No you aren't.

"Yes I am—I'd like to take a look at this commune bathroom so yes I am coming with you."

B. Lynn scuffs down the hall behind Franny O'Brien until she notices her bare feet are gorging themselves on splinters from the sagging wood floor. She switches to high-stepping because hobbling around on porcupine feet would likely ruin her entire summer. But it's been a long time since she last saw a porcupine so she doesn't know for sure if they actually waddle around on top of their prickers or if their feet are naked.

She asks Franny O'Brien when was the last time she saw a porcupine and Franny O'Brien stops cold and says, *What.*

"I was wondering if you've seen a porcupine recently."

Franny O'Brien breathes, *Jesus* and continues walking down the hall so B. Lynn figures she's through with this conversation.

"I wouldn't take a bath in that greasy-ass thing," B. Lynn says leaning over Franny O'Brien and peering into the bathtub.

I don't hear anyone asking you to. Get away from me you feel like a damned postage stamp stuck on my back or some kind of runty rodent. Give me some decent privacy for a few minutes would you I can't even breathe.

B. Lynn says, "Good luck with your privacy" and walks out of the bathroom.

She is high-stepping down the hall when the flipped-out guy thrusts his head out a door and says, *Where's my shit.*

"Your shit's on our bed right where you threw it. Go get it we don't want it in our room—why can't you keep it in your own room."

The flipped-out guy says, *Just hang onto it for me will ya* and slams the door. A few minutes later he crashes into B. Lynn's room and says, *I need my shit man like right now.*

"Good we don't want it in here—why are you dragging your dirty underpants around."

What the fuck—I told you it's my shit man. He grabs his sack and charges out the door.

The next thing cops are pounding on doors and walls and yelling, *Raid! Everybody open up.* B. Lynn's door is already open so she doesn't have to do what the cops say. One of them steps into her room and looks at her. He doesn't say anything and neither does she and then he leaves and pretty soon it's quiet.

Franny O'Brien finally comes back wafting patchouli and B. Lynn asks if she enjoyed her privacy.

Where's that guy's sack.

"He came and got it."

Good we didn't want it in here.

"No. We really didn't."

Did he say what's in it?

"Uh-huh. He said it was his shit."

Franny O'Brien is quiet for a moment and then says *Oh. It was his SHIT. Well. He could have shared it.*

Pit Stop

Franny O'Brien squats in the weeds, her back turned to the cows gathered morosely in a field across the road. B. Lynn stands, arms and legs spread wide to shield her from nothing. It is too hard for B. Lynn not to yell CAR!—so she yells, "CAR!" Franny O'Brien, crouched over, jumps like a toad poked with a stick and pees into her underpants and they laugh so hard she pees all over her feet, too.

No longer laughing, she paces straddle-legged, fanning her hands at the crotch of her blue jeans because *What if somebody decides to drive down this god-forsaken bitch of a road and has the goddam DECENCY to give us a ride and then I go and leave a pee stain on the seat of their car—what would you think about somebody who did that—what would you think about somebody who left pee all over the inside of your car after you had the goddam decency to give them a ride.* B. Lynn doesn't know what she'd think about somebody who left pee all over the inside of her car because she's never owned one.

They are neither here nor there; they are nowhere but eleven miles back from where they had been when a state trooper suggested they march a specific part of their bodies straight to the bus station. They had assured him that taking a bus was an excellent idea, uh-huh, and why hadn't they thought about that. He told them he would be coming back to make sure they understood exactly why they should have thought about that.

Ride a bus? That requires money, of which they have little. That requires common sense, of which they have none. Since they couldn't make any progress moving forward, they crossed the road to go backward and caught a ride that carried them past scenery too familiar and they were damn near back home:

"Sir, would you mind, could you please—STOP THE CAR." Crossing the road, they again turned to go back to where they had been.

They sing, *Hot town summer in the city back of my neck getting dirty and gritty* and wish they had some Southern Comfort so they could swill it and then smash the empty bottle on the ground. With their toes they draw the initials of boys they love in the roadside dirt, B. Lynn marking the same two letters she's been writing for the last four years.

Franny O'Brien stands, hands on hips, and glares at the empty expanse of road that stretches out like a long skinny skunk dead in a shimmer of heat. B. Lynn joins her and they dance on burning feet, tar bubbling up and sticking to their toes that they will pick at for the rest of the summer. They sit in the grass and chew on weeds, tangy and bitter.

A car blows past, little kids in the back seat scramble around to stare wide-eyed at them through the rear window. One of them waves.

They belt-out 'Ninety-Nine Bottles of Beer on the Wall' and wish for a long cool drink of water; they fiddle around with the pearl tops of the hatpins they carry woven in the cloth of their jeans, weapons to poke out the eyeballs of anyone who tries to get funny.

B. Lynn dozes in the sun while Franny O'Brien bitches because her fair skin is starting to burn, looking like she's plunged her face into a pot of boiling water, she's starving, she's dammit-all soggy and starting to stink and *Whose idea was this for chrissakes.*

Hearing the low hum of a car growing louder, they scramble to the edge of the road and flick out their thumbs. Franny O'Brien yells, *Are you fucking KIDDING ME* when the car slices through the wavy image of moisture in the distance and then disappears.

The sun shifts west, their shadows stretch longer. Franny O'Brien flops back in the grass and blows out a heavy insinuating sigh. B. Lynn cautiously clears her throat and lightly taps her fingers to the beat of an endless song sliding around in her head, whining cicadas the only sound disturbing the heated silence.

They contemplate their situation. They contemplate each other. Only a slight bend keeps B. Lynn from being completely straight, but she looks addicted—Squeaky Fromme-ish—hair cut so short because everyone else grows theirs so long, eyes dark from too many sleepless nights and too many diets. Franny O'Brien has long blonde hair and looks reasonable.

Franny O'Brien stands alone beside the road, smiling her Catholic schoolgirl smile and looking blonde. A car screams past, careens and skids to a stop sending up a shower of dust and gravel. It slowly backs up. B. Lynn pops out of the weeds and trots after Franny O'Brien who is definitely going to leave a pee stain on the seat of the car.

Rain

B. Lynn squints through the screen door of her basement apartment at Shirley and she isn't happy with the sight of her. She doesn't know Shirley all that well but she's heard plenty about her, so she knows her well enough. B. Lynn opens the door and pokes out her head to look up at the sky and sees that it is a splendid spring day and then she looks back at unsightly Shirley who bears a slight resemblance to Janis Joplin without the cool.

So whadduya #@%* think? Do you wannna go to the %$#@ concert or %!# what? Shirley's language makes B. Lynn's ears pucker-up and crawl inside her head. Although she has her own repertoire of indecent words, she grew up in Fair Field, New York, so she knows there is a line of demarcation between good-natured foul mouthery and blatant vulgarity. Shirley has not had the advantage of a Fair Field education.

After a few minutes of sifting through Shirley's word dirt, B. Lynn discovers she is being invited to hitchhike to a three-day outdoor concert in Scandia, Pennsylvania. She is not inclined to go anywhere with Shirley and she is also right in the middle of a particularly fine book. But it has been a tiresome week of waiting for her roommates to return from spring break—they wanted to go home for chrissakes—and all the waiting, reading and wondering why anyone would want to go home for chrissakes is wearing on her nerves. She looks at Shirley and feels queasy, looks back up at the splendid spring day and feels better, so she decides to go to Scandia, Pennsylvania.

They arrive at a struggling imitation of Woodstock right along with rolling black clouds and the first mutterings of thunder. B. Lynn worries about lightning, electrocution and

Shirley, who is already behaving in a manner that supports everything she has heard about her.

Shirley pushes through the crowd, bouncing and bleating at boys who look as if they've lurched out of the Ozark Mountains, rather than the hills of Pennsylvania. She eventually finds a group of inbred looking creatures who don't care that she is Shirley; she grabs one by the arm and drags him into a tent. B. Lynn sits on the ground and listens to defective loud speakers crackle noise created by defective musicians.

The clouds rip open, relieving themselves of a deluge of rain. B. Lynn hunches over to protect her face with her knees and worries about lightning, electrocution and worms. She doesn't worry about Shirley because she is being well taken care of. A boy pokes her on the shoulder and offers to share his blanket. She rolls her eyes and shakes her head and the boy says, *I'm only asking if you want to share a BLANKET for chrissakes.* So she crawls under his blanket because he's short and so is she, and he also has a bottle of Boone's Farm and a package of Oreos.

She spends the filthy night trying to keep her distance from the boy, yet still remain under his blanket that smells of old dogs or maybe feet. He was honorable, sharing only his blanket—never once offering to share himself or anything else. B. Lynn is glad he didn't try to share himself, but she would have liked some wine and cookies.

Morning yawns and then falls back into deep slumber, defeated by clouds and rain. B. Lynn slogs through mud, ignoring cordial offers of hospitality under blankets, looking for Shirley. When she finds her she wishes she hadn't, because Shirley is more unsightly than a person should ever be. And she plans on remaining that way for two more days.

B. Lynn would rather yank off her own head than spend another night under an old dog blanket—and she might not be able to find the boy who didn't offer to share himself because she won't recognize him without his Boone's Farm and Oreos. She remembers her particularly fine book, home alone and waiting for her, so decides to leave Scandia, Pennsylvania— which is a very good place to leave Shirley.

Standing by the side of a dirt road in descending dusk, she sticks out her thumb and hopes she isn't heading in the wrong direction because she has a habit of heading in the wrong direction. In a spray of mud and gravel a car stops, impossibly stuffed with boys. B. Lynn backs up a few steps and waves them on. One of them yells, *We won't fucking bother you.* Edging closer to the car, she can tell from their red heavy-lidded eyes they probably aren't capable of bothering her. She accepts the ride even though she is concerned they might have split personalities: their long hair is indicative of hippies, but their baseball caps are indicative of rednecks.

Squeezing into the corner of the back seat, she leans her head against the window. She stares at the verdure of trees and hills passing dim behind a veil of rain and thinks about her book.

Combat Zone

Dublinski thinks she might need a salt tablet from one of the medics running reconnaissance for unconscious bodies in the crowd, but she isn't sure. She asks B. Lynn to feel for aridity on her forehead even though she knows B. Lynn has issues about touching other people's foreheads—especially one that hasn't been washed for a couple of days and has a hot pimple protruding from the middle of it.

B. Lynn reluctantly presses a finger onto Dublinski's forehead—she is offering it up like a Sunday ham festooned with a cherry—and tells her she is sweating for chrissakes and people don't sweat when there isn't any fluid left in their bodies.

Holding her finger up in the air, disgusting with Dublinski's forehead slime, B. Lynn worries about how she's going to wash the damn thing because she's sitting in a simmering swamp of humanity somewhere in Washington, D.C. where it's hotter than Hanoi. The city officials hadn't thought to provide washroom facilities for the thousands of civic-minded college students visiting the Capitol to yell about stuff and tip over police cars in order to end the war in Vietnam. Dublinski insists she's feeling faint—nauseous too—and B. Lynn tells her the medics have run out of water to chase down the damned salt tablets–had she thought about that? Dublinski hadn't thought about that so she curls into a fetal position and falls asleep, bothering people around her because there isn't enough room for fetal positions without intruding on someone else's piece of grass.

She creates a domino effect: people scoot forward on their rear-ends to accommodate Dublinski, rippling all the way up to the stage where Jane Fonda is blathering about Cambodia or some such place.

B. Lynn slumps, fretting about her finger and listening to people grumble about Dublinski who is sleeping like a baby during these Important Times and this Serious Business of sitting righteously knees-to-elbows in order to end the war in Vietnam. Dublinski is roused from her nap when everyone starts chanting: *KENT STATE—KENT STATE* and passing limp dollar bills up to Jane Fonda for the kids who were killed by kids with nervous fingers. B. Lynn can't figure how money is going to help them now. Anyway, she doesn't have a dollar for Jane Fonda and neither does Dublinski who has to go to the bathroom.

They trip over land mines of body parts—what with all the toes and fingers underfoot—some people swear at them but some people say, *Peace, man* and B. Lynn wonders which one of them looks like a man.

All the restaurants have penciled signs hanging in their windows that say 'No Hippies Allowed.' Dublinski would just as soon pee on the sidewalk but for all the soldier kids brandishing sticks and dirty looks. Also, B. Lynn reminds her they slept on the sidewalk the night before and if they can't catch a ride home they might be sleeping there again. And if everyone pees on the sidewalk, where the hell are they going to find a decent place to sleep for chrissakes—had she thought about that? Dublinski hadn't thought about that—so they go in a parking garage and she pees behind a car.

Battle-fatigued, they lie on their backs under a tree to gather their strength before fighting their way back through the jungle of people. A raggedy-ass boy strolls over and asks if they want Mary Jane and Dublinski sharply refuses. B. Lynn, never knowing what to say about anything, rolls her eyes and says nothing.

The boy shrugs and walks away, leaving Dublinski and B. Lynn discussing what there is about them that would make him think they might be interested in fooling around with some chick named Mary Jane.

Riding home with a couple of guys, they stop at a roadside park where somebody is cooking hot dogs and they hear that a kid they know got tear-gassed. Dublinski and B. Lynn feel dispirited because they didn't get tear-gassed or need any salt tablets, and they are pretty sure they must look like lesbians. But they are proud they have done their part to end the war in Vietnam.

Taking Orders

Harry the cook is dripping lunchtime rush sweat onto the hamburger and French fries he's arranging on a plate. B. Lynn is mesmerized as she watches another droplet slalom down his forehead, traverse the bridge of his nose and then hesitate on the tip, before free-falling and landing on the soft hamburger bun.

He shoves the plate across the stainless steel counter and yells, *Pick it up and get it the hell out of here.* B. Lynn grabs the plate and settles it on her tray, feeling glad she isn't the one who will be eating that soggy old bun. As she turns to race back to the dining room the hamburger and French fries tap dance off the plate, kiss the tray goodbye and scatter across the floor.

She stares at the hamburger and French fries, stunned by their acrobatic performance, until Harry yells, *Pick it up and get it the hell out of here.* B. Lynn swivels back to the counter grateful for his foresight—having another dish already prepared in case she dropped the first one—but, with the exception of a lingering French fry, the counter is bare. Harry yells, *I said pick it up and get it the hell out of here.*

B. Lynn glances back at the food on the floor and then at Harry. She quickly stoops down and uses her hands to sweep the French fries into a pile; she uses the plate as a dust pan to scoop them up. The hamburger and top bun had hugged each other close during their hasty bail-out, but the bottom bun had apparently decided to run like hell to get away from the crash site.

Crawling around on her hands and knees B. Lynn eventually discovers the bottom bun cowering under the meat freezer. She picks off bits of under-the-meat-freezer stuff from the bun and then tucks it beneath the hamburger and top bun. Standing up with the reconditioned food disarranged on the plate she looks at Harry again, not entirely convinced he believes she should serve a meal fresh off the kitchen floor. But he yells, *Get it the hell out of here* so she quickly gets it the hell out of there.

Sidling past Harry's mother, the Waitress Nazi, she dashes through the dining room and plunks down the plate in front of a gentleman unaware of the tragic history of his food. He is eager for a good gobble so B. Lynn figures his mouth probably won't notice it's eating kitchen floor food. She wonders if his stomach will.

Turning away from the grateful gobbler, she is struck dumb with terror. While she was mopping the kitchen floor with hamburger buns and French fries, a population explosion occurred in her section of the dining room. She blinks rapidly and counts the tables: "One, two, three, five—no—one, two, four, six—NO. One. Two. Three. Four. Five. Six. Seven. SEVEN?!"

The Waitress Nazi stumps up behind her and hisses, *You have orders to pick up in the kitchen.*

A Waitress Comrade brushes past her and snaps, *I had to pick up your frigging orders in the kitchen.*

B. Lynn jerks into action and rushes from one table to the next: "May I take your order?—May I take your order?—What kind of food do you want."

She hustles back to the kitchen, her notepad crammed with scribblings: *1ch burger hold ch add mNN≠uWsh & fr on 2 3 4salads/ 1 Aor cr/ 1 &no let add spin & anch—1 steak well— not burned/ hold ff/ +add bk pot no sr crm butter*

Harry yells, *Where the hell have you been?*

"Taking orders!"

What the hell took you so long.

B. Lynn yells, "I was taking a lot of orders!"—and slaps her notepad onto the counter. Harry snatches the notepad, flips through the pages, and then slaps it back at B. Lynn.

Who the hell taught you how to take orders!

B. Lynn thinks for a moment. She says, "Well. My parents tried... and some teachers. But I've just never been very good at taking anyone's orders."

Trip

B. Lynn clutches the receiver and slides down the glass wall of the telephone booth. Crouching in a rustling mess of gum wrappers and cigarette butts, she stretches the phone cord until there is enough to wrap tightly around her wrist. She adjusts the receiver more snugly against her ear and says, "What? Mom—what? What did you say?"

I said, the Short Italian Kid called here last week and asked for you.

"Well. What did he want?"

Beats me.

It beats B. Lynn, too. It beats her for the remainder of the summer and into the fall: she pokes and prods at the implications of that phone call like a sore tooth. She can't figure any reason why a boy she hasn't softened her eyes on in two years—a boy who hasn't said a single word to her in four years—a boy who has disturbed her heart and exhausted her with the loving of him from a distance for five years—would call her on the telephone.

That solitary phone call might have been enough to snare B. Lynn's future but it is her friend Smith, with all her goading and testing of B. Lynn's mettle, who sets the packing tape to unrolling, sticky side ready to seal her life up tight.

The Short Italian Kid is home on leave from the navy. Smith says.

"So."

So call him up.

"No."

Find out what he wanted.

"Don't care."

I'll look up his phone number.

"I said NO for chrissakes."

*Do you remember what you said when we were fifteen—
you said you were going to marry him someday. Ha! You didn't
even know him. So probably he called to ask you to get
married.*

"You're really very funny. Do you know that? You are
absolutely very hysterical. Christ."

B. Lynn is perfectly content wandering around in her life—
not bothering anybody but herself—and she is not inclined to
call any boys up especially not the Short Italian Kid because
she knows—Smith was breathless with the telling of it—that
the night before a skinny girl with long hair presented him with
roses at the bowling alley. The skinny girl is in love with him
and he is a big deal home on leave from the navy in his dress
whites— which makes the skinny girl with the flowers a big
deal, too. B. Lynn is never skinny enough, she doesn't have
long hair or any roses, but Smith is aggravating her and she's
braver when she's aggravated, so she calls him:

"Hi. So. My mom said you called me last summer."

Who is this?

"This is B. Lynn. My mom said you called me."

I did. Yes! I did call you. So what are you doing?

B. Lynn asks, "With my life or right now?"—as she
stretches out her leg to kick Smith who is wallowing around on
the floor and snorting like a pig in fresh mud because she
knows B. Lynn is making a complete ass of herself.

He says, *Tonight.*

B. Lynn repeats, "Tonight"—and the next thing she knows
they are at the Elbow Room Bar and Grill sitting at a plank
table scarred with initials and obscenities and For a good time
call Rosa drinking warm draft beer out of plastic cups and
talking and talking about books and they agree they must be

soul mates because they have both read 'Big Phil's Kid' and they have never met anyone else who has read 'Big Phil's Kid.'

He returns to his naval station on a submarine, she returns to college, and they exchange long impassioned letters that are mutually complimentary. He thinks she is a fine writer and she thinks he is a fine writer and they have both read 'Big Phil's Kid,' so they decide to get married.

His parents think this is a marvelous plan because he is out of his mind and out of control and they think B. Lynn will provide a good and calming influence. Because she is very quiet about it, they don't realize she is also out of her mind and out of control. Her parents think this is a marvelous plan because they are just plain tired of her and it would be nice to have the Short Italian Kid have a turn getting just plain tired of her.

Four months later, he wears his brother's too large suit and B. Lynn scrounges a dress. They say their vows sneaking silly faces at each other—this is all such a lark—and as they walk down the aisle—both twenty years old, still a boy and still a girl—B. Lynn says, "I can't cook, I won't sew and I don't clean ovens." He finds this remarkably funny and so they are laughing as they walk out of the church into the sunshine.

But B. Lynn trips on the slated steps of the church and falls right into the next nine years—when nothing is remarkably funny.

Perfectly Crazy

The Short Italian Kid thinks B. Lynn should be called Sally and he could be called Fritzel. So that's what they call each other: Sally and Fritzel. Sally is in college choking on Chaucer, Fritzel is a cook in the Navy on a defunct diesel sub—the last of its kind—spooning up slop for sailors with nowhere to go.

Fritzel thinks Sally should marry him. He thinks they could be called Sally and Fritzel Frizzo. Sally marries him because she can—she always knew she would—and he was her ticket to ride. Also, they wear the same size clothes and he has better blue jeans. They are a perfect fit.

There is a wedding reception of sorts at some restaurant with his parents and her parents. They eat steaks and drink drinks. Her mother makes a toast—she is enjoying the drinks—she says: *Call me crazy—and I might be crazy—but two twenty-year-old kids tangled together forever is perfectly crazy.*

Sally's father says, *Jesus.*

Fritzel's parents clink spoons on wine glasses, tinkling noise to fill up empty awkwardness. Also, they would like to see some kissing. Sally and Fritzel know each other well but it is uncomfortable kissing in front of too many parents. They laugh inside each other's mouths.

The wedding celebration is kind of depressing—it is kind of a drag—it is a bit of a bore. Sally and Fritzel want to get moving—they need to get going—they itch with the wanting and they're nervous with the needing: they have three days and two thousand miles to outrun Fritzel's Absence with Leave. He has been Absent without Leave, to love Sally, too much.

Sally and Fritzel think their car should be called Thelonious: Thelonious Frizzo. So that's what they call him.

Thelonious Frizzo is a purple Pinto with digestive disorders. He breaks wind and sometimes chokes on his own gas.

Sally and Fritzel and other sundry stuff, stuff into Thelonious Frizzo and they get going south, slide-stepping to Poughkeepsie: Fritzel wants Sally to get a look at his grandparents and they want to get a look at her.

Fritzel's grandpa is called Po-Po and his grandma is called Mo-Mo—also, there is Uncle Frank. They are Po-Po and Mo-Mo Figarelli and Uncle Frank. Everybody looks at everybody and Uncle Frank says, *How do you do.*

Sally has a cough caught in her throat. It wracks her ribs— her head—and the house. Po-Po is a doctor, a collector of needles. He wants to shoot Sally in her rear-end with one of his needles cocked and loaded with penicillin and so he does. Sally is embarrassed having her new Po-Po inspect her rear- end and she doesn't feel any better for it.

Mo-Mo is short—she's shorter than Fritzel—shorter than Sally—shorter than anybody. Her shortness consists of one big bosom draped to her knees. Mo-Mo keeps an opened jar of mayonnaise in the kitchen cupboard. Sally thinks Po-Po and Mo-Mo are a little dangerous.

It is raining slick and silvery in West Virginia, Thelonious hisses and shocks open his eyes. Sally thinks they should stop and take off their clothes. She thinks they could run wild and free in the woods in the rain—and maybe sit on a rock. She has read about that—someone did that—in a book. Maybe 'Lady Chatterley's Lover.'

Fritzel says: *Call me crazy—and I might be crazy—but behaving brazenly bare-assed in broad day-light is perfectly crazy.* He veers onto a random road anyway, to do Sally's thing. But Sally decides she's not in the right kind of mood to be wet—she's not in the right kind of mood to sit on a rock—

she's not in the right kind of mood for Fritzel—but she is in the right kind of mood to be wild and free. Maybe.

At a rest stop in Kentucky Fritzel is tripping on tiredness. He says, *Baby, you can drive my car.*

Sally says, "Baby, I don't know how to drive your car."

Fritzel says, *It's so easy.* Sally steers Thelonious Frizzo down Route One nearing ninety and fiddling with frequencies—the radio waves vacant with Country and Western static.

Fritzel sleeps wound wedged with a fern fondling his ear, making love to his nose. A shirt box filled with homemade cookies is his pillow. Fritzel is crumbly when he wakes up. They eat oatmeal cookies plucked from his hair.

Blowing through Georgia, furnace air blasts and pummels their faces through Thelonious Frizzo's yawning windows. It snatches at Fritzel's curls making him look like he has a wad of the wrong kind of hair stuck on his forehead. It is fun calling him Wad, Wad Frizzo, but not for long.

In Titusville Fritzel is tormented with a troublesome tooth, an insistent incisor. It bosses his brain—it makes him punch right-fisted on the steering wheel—skittering Thelonious Frizzo sideways like a horse with a novice rider.

The tooth tells Fritzel to punch left-fisted on the steering wheel to straighten Thelonious Frizzo out—and suggests maybe Sally could use some straightening out, too. The tooth tells Fritzel to stomp on the gas— stomp on the brake—tear at his hair and swear. The tooth yells, *Fuck this shit.*

Sally mutters, "Christ."

The tooth screams, *Fuck you, too,* skidding Thelonious Frizzo to a shuddering, stuttering—stop.

Rummaging in Thelonious Frizzo's rear end, Fritzel grabs just the tool to teach his tooth a thing or two. Sally prefers not to learn a thing or two. He plunges the pliers into his mouth—

yanks the terrible tooth out of his head and spits. Sally stares at the tooth dead in the dirt. She worries there might be more malignant molars living in Fritzel's mouth.

Thelonious Frizzo bridges Sally and Fritzel over the Florida Keys heading south of south, surrounded by water. Sally notices there is no stopping—no escaping—the water—the heat—or Fritzel. She nibbles her first second thought, she thinks: "Call me crazy—and I might be crazy—but Fritzel is perfectly hellishly crazy."

Indigestion

Fritzel is careening through college—he is high on college and working hard at growing his hair. It is 1973, he is on the back-end cusp of *Far Out* so he has to grow it fast. He has to have fun, fast, too. He is living so high and fast sometimes he is called Fast Fritzel.

Fritzel is flitting around near the ceiling because he is so high and fast. His boyfriends, Blowfish Bob and Facially Disfigured Dick, are also flitting around near the ceiling. They live with Sally and Fritzel because they enjoy being fast with Fritzel and he loves being fast with them. He believes Sally will come to love Blowfish Bob and Facially Disfigured Dick as much as he does.

Sally doesn't get involved in being high and fast; she watches Fritzel being high and fast. But her stomach can't stomach her head watching Fritzel spin like a dime on edge, and her stomach yells to her head, *Don't make me come up there.* Sally eats some crackers and hopes her stomach doesn't choke on them.

Her head and stomach continue to be confrontational so she calls a doctor up, she say, "Doctor, ain't there nothin' I can take"—she say, "Doctor, to relieve this belly ache."

The doctor, he say, *See me in the morning and I'll tell you what to do.*

So Sally goes to the doctor and the doctor, he say, *You got a baby lime in your coconut—there ain't nothing you can take, to relieve this bellyache.* Sally is alarmed because she knows it's a bad idea—it isn't a good idea—for a lime to hang around growing up, when she and Fritzel are still hanging around growing up.

But when she say to Fritzel, "You puts a lime in my coconut," he claps his hands and kisses the ceiling because he is excited about seeing more kinds of himself running around. Sally and Fritzel decide to call the lime Wumpo: Wumpo Frizzo. It seems like a good kind of name for somebody they don't know. Sally continues growing Wumpo, Fritzel continues growing his hair, Blowfish Bob and Facially Disfigured Dick continue growing annoying.

***

Sally perches on the edge of her bed looking like Buddha with stringy hair. She wishes she was somewhere other than inside her own body because the insides of her own body are acting as if they would rather be somewhere else, too. She shoves off the side of the bed and fumbles down the stairs to the kitchen.

Blowfish Bob and Facially Disfigured Dick are lounging at the kitchen table, having so much fast fun at three o'clock in the morning they forgot to go to bed. Blowfish Bob squints at Sally, slowly spiraling fun out of his mouth and she doesn't know which is more distasteful: Blowfish Bob looking like Blowfish Bob, or Blowfish Bob looking like a smoldering trash fire.

Stretching across the table to reach the telephone on the kitchen counter, she leans over Facially Disfigured Dick causing her lime, Wumpo, to plump against his head. The plumping makes him think of marshmallows; he would very much like some marshmallows. He asks Sally what she thinks about them. She is not inclined to answer. He becomes contemplative and then says he'd settle for some Rice Crispy treats. He asks Sally what she thinks about them.

Sally calls the doctor, woke him up—she say, "Doctor, ain't there nothing I can take" she say, "Doctor, to relieve my worser belly ache."

The doctor, he say, *The lime in your coconut it ain't going wait*—he say, *Go on to the hospital before it's too late.*

Using the hand rail as a tow rope, Sally hauls herself back up the stairs to her bedroom.

She stares at the Fritzel lump breathing in the bed and then shoves his shoulder. Fritzel, sleeping like a lime, worn out from growing his hair, rolls over and snortles. Sally shoves his shoulder with a little more intent and Fritzel says, *Christ.*

Sally doesn't like the tone of his snortle and she doesn't like the tone of his *Christ* so she shoves his head. She say, "Take me to the hospital before it's too late."

Sally waddles into the hospital and a lime nurse skates a wheelchair toward her. Sally worries the last person to sit in it might have been an old person with a gaping hospital gown; she shuffles backward and collides with Fritzel who is having an orientation problem.

The lime nurse lemons her lips and says riding in the wheelchair is a rule. Sally doesn't like rules and she doesn't mind in the least about breaking them. Shrinking past the wheelchair, she asks to be shown to her room. She wonders if she's supposed to give the nurse a tip.

Lying in a bed in a room that is aesthetically displeasing, a different lime nurse, in gestures of reassurance, bangs Sally on the forehead with a hand that looks like a slab of ham. She asks if there is anything else Sally needs and Sally says she needs something to read. The nurse gazes at her, thinking maybe Sally has escaped from the psych floor. But she bustles away and returns with a 'Reader's Digest.'

Sally is just settling in to read about humorous uniforms when the lime doctor stumps in, peevish because Sally called him, woke him up. His shirt is needled with short slivers of hair, making her suspect he's been rolling around on the floor with a dog. It occurs to her that he might actually be a veterinarian—and if that's the case, she wishes she hadn't let him see her stuff.

The doctor bungles under Sally's blanket then retracts his head like a startled turtle. He say, *The lime in your coconut, it ain't going to wait.* The nurse snatches Sally's 'Reader's Digest' and Sally lunges to grab it back—she's not going anywhere without something to read. The lunging encourages Wumpo to pop out onto the bed. She looks more like a squalling purple prune than a lime.

Running Out of Time

An ocean wave carrying Sally's Fresh Lime Froggy crests and then crashes inside her belly. Fritzel tells her to breathe through her mouth. After the wave slides into shore Sally tells Fritzel to breathe through his ass-hole. She looks at Fritzel and thinks, *Asshole.*

Rolling onto her side, Sally squints through the railing of her hospital bed. The narrowing of her view smudges away the rest of the room giving the effect of being closed into a small space with Fritzel. She quickly releases her eyelids when she notices the bars on the railing look just like the bars of a prison cell and Fritzel, slouched in a chair next to the bed, looks just like a warden.

Sally cradles her weighted balloon of a belly and rocks back and forth to gain enough momentum to move onto her back: like a sluggish cement mixer she slowly rolls over, feeling Fresh Lime Froggy pummeling her insides as she scrambles to come with her. She stares up at the ceiling. Her eyes grab onto the black dots peppered on the acoustic tiles and begin arranging them into interesting patterns. One of Wumpo's bunny slippers slides into focus and just as she notices a water stain profile of Jimmy Carter another wave surges, this one spiraling her right down to the bottom of the ocean.

Coming up for air, Sally keeps her eyes closed as she waits for another suggestion from Fritzel about the fundamentals of breathing when you're drowning. But he only hums, a flat-line hum with a point. It spears out of his nostrils until it reaches the far wall. It turns and coils. Taking aim, the hum shoots straight out and bores a hole right in the center of Sally's forehead.

Sally would like Fritzel to be involved in something challenging, so she shuffles her head sideways on the mash of pillows and tells him to hum Jimi Hendrix's version of the 'Star Spangled Banner,' because she knows it is impossible to hum Jimi Hendrix's version of the 'Star Spangled Banner.' To accommodate the bending notes of the guitar he would have to open his mouth which would be singing, and it would be exciting to wait for Fritzel to open his mouth so she can tell him he's not humming, he's singing.

Fritzel is quiet as he considers the intricacies of the song, and then folds his arms and taps his foot in the steady rhymeless beat of a leaking gutter on a drizzly day. Sally gazes back up at the ceiling and watches as one of the dots forms into a water droplet. It lingers and wobbles before plinking down into the humming hole in her forehead.

A wave suddenly churns-up sludge from the floor of Sally's belly and becomes a mud slide roiling toward a breach in the dam. She tells Fritzel it's time and Fritzel says it isn't time. He says it is still morning and the doctor promised they had a whole day and into the evening worth of time. Sally tells Fritzel that Fresh Lime Froggy apparently doesn't know how to tell time—that maybe he should find a doctor or nurse so they can teach Fresh Lime Froggy all about doing things at the right time.

Fritzel stands, twists his head around until his neck cracks and then strolls to the door. He looks left, he looks right; he looks at the floor. He turns and tells Sally he can't find a doctor or a nurse. Feeling as if there's a plunger sucking Fresh Lime Froggy's head in and out in and out of her body Sally yells, "Then find a damned janitor for chrissakes."

Bending into the hallway, Fritzel flirts his hand back and forth in a beauty queen kind of way and displays his teeth in a rictus kind of way. A nurse, impersonating a giant marshmallow with a paper coffee filter perched on its head, plumps into the room and Sally gags, having a particular aversion at that moment to nurses who look like giant marshmallows.

Keeping his mouth stretched wide and talking behind his teeth, Fritzel leans toward the marshmallow and tells her a secret. He punctuates the end of his secret with *heh-heh-heh* so she will understand he is the only one in the room who knows how to tell time. The marshmallow replies, *Heh-heh-heh* because it makes her feely cozy.

Sticky-footing across the floor to Sally's bed, she flips the sheet up with the back of her hand while keeping her eyes on Fritzel, so they can continue their friendly *heh-heh-heh* chat. She glances down at Sally—*Heh-heh-HELL.*

Ramming Sally's bed around the room as if it's a grocery cart with a wayward wheel, the marshmallow jerks to a stop before crashing out the door and down the hall to the delivery room. She tells Sally to give Fritzel a kiss goodbye. The marshmallow doesn't know Sally gave him his kiss goodbye nine months ago. Turning her head away, Sally thinks what she thinks about Fritzel.

It's a Good Thing

Once upon a time in the Land of Goody-Two-Shoes, there lived a wicked witch. The witch didn't mind that people thought her wicked because it served to frighten away evil spirits and hateful demons. She lived many years happy and content with just the company of her two lovely young daughters, whom she nurtured and protected because they were the best parts of her life.

Across the Land of Goody-Two-Shoes there lived a gallant man in a dark and dank cellar. He had two handsome young sons, whom he nurtured and protected because they were the best parts of his life.

When the witch's older daughter reached her tenth year, the witch sent a message to her Place of Learning requesting a teacher of male gender. The witch did this because her daughter had only known men who were loathsome toads and rapscallions, and she wished her daughter to know that all men were not thus (although the witch secretly believed all men were thus).

And so it came to be in the following year, her daughter was instructed by a male teacher, who also happened to be the gallant man who lived in a dark and dank cellar across the Land of Goody-Two-Shoes. The witch's daughter flourished under his guidance, and she was happy and not afraid.

One ordinary day of ordinary things, the witch noticed her daughter had forgotten to take her noon meal to her Place of Learning. Snatching up the brown paper sack, the witch scurried to deliver the meal to her daughter so she would not know hunger.

As the witch was taking leave of her daughter's classroom in the Place of Learning, to continue her ordinary day of ordinary things, the gods winked and sprinkled an extra dose of courage down upon her head. They winked and sprinkled an extra dose of courage down upon the gallant man's head, as well.

Spurred on with his extra dose of courage, the gallant man dashed from the classroom and pursued the witch down echoing corridors. Just as she was flitting out the door he caught the witch and begged the pleasure of her company for his evening meal. With her extra dose of courage, the witch promised to bestow upon him the pleasure of her company. They were both privately bemused about their agreement because she had sworn off men, and he had sworn off witches.

Their meal together was a grand success and they both thought, *This might be a good thing.* They continued to see each other, despite the warnings and despair of the gallant man's many henchmen who tore at their own hair and moaned that the witch would lead him to nothing but trouble and heartache.

The day came when the gallant man and the witch thought to inquire the name of the other. The gallant man replied that he was known as Mr. Smith. The witch said although she had been called many things, most recently Sally, her given name was B. Lynn.

With the formality of names concluded, they decided to introduce his handsome young sons to her lovely young daughters. They watched as their children took great delight in each other—especially the younger son and younger daughter who shared the same first name. As the children frolicked and laughed, Mr. Smith and B. Lynn looked at each other and thought, *This might be a good thing.*

And so it came to pass shortly thereafter, in the magical month of October when winds quicken and fairies show themselves, Mr. Smith and B. Lynn were united in marriage and the two families became one.

The years that followed were busy ones, indeed. The parents and children rushed about to athletic contests demonstrating their valor and strength and good character. They purchased a dwelling that was filled with noise and gladness. They played games, explored other lands in faraway places; they celebrated joyous Christmases and very happy birthdays. And in all the commotion, Mr. Smith and B. Lynn looked at each other and thought, *This is a good thing.*

Eventually the children grew up and left to seek their own fortunes in the world. Even though Mr. Smith and B. Lynn knew it was the right way of all things, they missed them dreadfully. But the children often returned to their home; the sons traveling great distances, the daughters not so far.

During their visits the house was once again filled with noise and boisterous happiness, because the children still delighted in each other's company. When they departed to continue pursuing their dreams Mr. Smith and B. Lynn still missed them, but they found they had come to enjoy their peace and quiet. They looked at each other and thought, *This is a good thing.*

The years whisked by with the speed of coursing greyhounds. When B. Lynn's older daughter brought home her own young gallant and asked Mr. Smith to escort her down the wedding aisle, Mr. Smith and B. Lynn looked at each other and thought, *This is a good thing.* When B. Lynn's younger daughter brought home her young gallant and asked Mr. Smith to walk her down the wedding aisle, Mr. Smith and B. Lynn looked at each other and thought, *This is a good thing.* As they held their first grandchild they both thought, *This is a good thing* and they thought that four more times.

Many years have passed, Mr. Smith and B. Lynn are growing old together. He is still a gallant man, but she retains the faint shadow of a witch: wicked words still tend to fly from her mouth like bats from a cave. He loves her and doesn't tell her the bloom of youth has faded from her cheeks. She loves him and doesn't tell him he repeats his stories. And they look at each other and know: *This is still a very good thing.*

B. Lynn Hopes Her Roots Aren't Showing

Although B. Lynn has soundly spanked her kneecaps, her legs still refuse to get out of the car. She tells the recalcitrant legs it's high time to wake up and take some responsibility for the rest of her body. She yells, "You've been sleeping for the last twelve hours—get up and make yourselves useful."

They grudgingly stir to life, whining about long road trips and how she isn't taking proper care of them—and she's pretty sure she hears her left leg make a snotty remark about her age. She says if they don't straighten up she's going to leave them alone in the hot car, provoking them to clamor about leg abuse and lawsuits. Because they're too lazy to exercise she sure as hell isn't going to have them expose their loose ways in front of a court room—there is nothing to do but drag them along behind her as she climbs out of the back seat.

Stepping down onto the cracked heat-waved driveway she staggers, haphazardly, because her feet are agitated about their sudden release from captivity: they race in little circles and then try to scoot off in different directions. Also, they are distracted by her legs who are calling them scabs and telling them they should join their strike—they might make signs— and B. Lynn hopes her heart isn't a member of the Leg Union. She stomps her feet and jumps up and down a couple of times so they will understand that, despite the chaos her legs are causing, she still runs the show.

Just as her legs and feet decide to behave appropriately, a water buffalo charges out the front door of her cousin's house. At the sight of the thing her feet skitter and her legs yell, *You didn't tell us they have PETS!* B. Lynn scatters her eyes around to find her sister, Soozie-Bells, so she can thrust her in the path of the water buffalo. Soozie-Bells is wearing a red shirt so the water buffalo would probably be more interested in engaging with her. But Soozie-Bells is still sitting in the car gazing despondently at her legs. She can't remember what to do with them and they aren't about to tell her.

As the water buffalo advances, B. Lynn realizes it is only Aunt Larlene with one of those 1960s parted-in-the-middle bouffant flip hairdos and B. Lynn is glad, as she has no use for water buffaloes. She doesn't yet know she isn't going to have much use for Aunt Larlene, either.

Aunt Larlene studies B. Lynn for a moment and then stabs her: *My golly you're just like your mother.* B. Lynn hasn't seen Aunt Larlene for thirty-two years so she wonders how she knows so damned much about her being just like her mother when she hasn't even had a chance to say anything nasty—and actually, it is Soozie-Bells who is just like their mother and she tells Larlene so. She is beginning to draw the comparisons of the objectionable behaviors between her sister and their mother, when she is engulfed in Aunt Larlene's stubby python arms.

Her welcoming hug feels like a backward Heimlich maneuver, making B. Lynn believe she might be choking and she doesn't know it because her brain isn't always aware of what the rest of her body is up to. She squirms around so Aunt Larlene can get her hands in the right place for thrusting—hoping she doesn't think the right place for thrusting is her neck. But Aunt Larlene only snuffles in the hair on the back of her head as if she's sniffing for the scent of more important relatives B. Lynn might have stopped to visit before coming to see her.

Just shy of shoving, she aims B. Lynn toward the house and prods her fingers in a hectic five-chord tune on her back. B. Lynn hums to the beat of the poking: Aunt Larlene is playing a vertebrae version of 'Boogie Woogie Bugle Boy'—a fine and invigorating song that makes her legs and feet happy they have come along.

The fingernail reveille propels her down a sidewalk tufting crabgrass, and guarded by garden gnomes that B. Lynn wants to kick because they look like runty clowns—if there is one thing she hates, it is a runty clown. She reaches out to twirl a listless whirly-gig waiting for a breath of a breeze, but Aunt Larlene yells, *DON'T TOUCH THAT* and changes her boogie-on-the-back recital to a flat-palmed-push.

She ushers B. Lynn up concrete steps in a crumbly mood and under an aluminum awning, haggardly hanging. B. Lynn looks up and notices a number of wind chimes with duct tape wrapped around their purposeful parts. She asks Aunt Larlene why they're bound and gagged and she replies, *Because they make too damned much noise.*

Yanking open the front screen door that has given up on keeping out flies, Aunt Larlene launches B. Lynn into smoldering darkness. It occurs to her that maybe she really had been choking out in the driveway and now she is dead and she yells, "Am I DEAD??"

The black heat feels as if the furnaces of hell are firing-up, but then she sees a light in the distance. As she moves toward the heavenly glow, arms outstretched, she tries to remember who is supposed to greet her—maybe Saint Peter.

Knocking into vicious obstacles that snag at her clothes and stumbling over bumps of stuff that might be small dogs—or maybe big rats—B. Lynn reminds herself the path to Jesus is not an easy one. But when she draws closer to the Presence, she discovers it is only a curly light bulb pooling a corona of stark white light over a musty molting pigeon crouching in a chair, in a corner: Ancient Auntie.

Ancient Auntie squints and pulls down her mouth, flipping through the card catalogue of her cobwebbed brain until she finds B. Lynn's number. Her jaw drops open like a ventriloquist's dummy and she coughs up word clots about her sister, B. Lynn's mother. Mucking through memory mud and dredging up years of spite, she spits, *Your mother—never—had to do a lick of work—like me and Larlene. Mamma called her Baby—when she was no more 'na baby—than I was. When she caught your Daddy and moved up north—she thought she was—pretty special—she thought she was—too good for us kids back home—she thought she was—Mrs. La—di—da.*

B. Lynn's breath chills her chest and freezes her lips: nobody's allowed to dish dirt about her mother, but her. She says, "Eighty-seven years—is a mighty long time—to store-up—so much—aggravation. You must be—exhausted."

B. Lynn is her mother's daughter.

***

Aunt Larlene's husband, Uncle Boy, lathers and gambols around the living room like an anxious puppy that doesn't know if it's going to get a belly rub or a kick in the head. Since they are meeting for the first time, B. Lynn doesn't know if it's appropriate to rub his belly or kick his head, so she pats his elbow. He seems to find that satisfying and B. Lynn feels encouraged that he didn't pee on her leg. He roots through heaps of newspapers, tangles of Christmas lights, and some blankets. Pawing the whole mess left, right and center, he makes Soozie-Bells and B. Lynn their own cozy sitting holes. He points to their designated holes and says, *Sit down and take some weight off your feet.* B. Lynn is flattered that he thinks her allotted space is big enough to accommodate her rear-end and pleased that he made Soozie-Bells' sitting hole larger than hers. Uncle Boy folds his arms and looks at them for a few minutes as though he is waiting to make sure they stay put. Content with their staying put, he wads himself up into a papasan chair and looks at them some more.

Aunt Larlene huffs and sprawls into her La-Z-Boy recliner and looks at them, too. There are a few minutes of everybody just looking. She finally says, *Did I tell you all I'm having me some moles burned off my back next month?*

B. Lynn doesn't quite know how to respond to that piece of information but Soozie-Bells says, *That's nice.* Ancient Auntie, glowering and moldering in her corner without a whole lot to say since B. Lynn set some conversational guidelines, ruffles her feathers and says, *It's a pity you all never found the time to come visit us sooner.*

Well Sister they're here now ain't they? says Aunt Larlene.

I suppose. Shifting her rustling rear-end around in the seat of her chair, Ancient Auntie suddenly perks up and says, *Your Granddad Elrod died right there on that sofa you're sitting on. It took us about fifteen bars of Lava soap to get all the blood off it. We almost wore our hands off. If you look real close you can still see some of it.*

Soozie-Bells gives a little snort—she always snorts when she's trying to control hysteria and it happens just before she starts crying—and B. Lynn hopes Granddad Elrod wasn't the last person to use the blanket that is piled next to her sitting hole.

A trembling TV tray holds a murky bowl that houses a hermit crab to marvel at. Aunt Larlene pontificates on the merits of owning a hermit crab—if you're going to have crabs that's the kind you want. Grunting her arm over the side of her chair, she flicks her fingers on the glass so her pet will get excited and show-off. Everyone watches it scuttle around for a few seconds before it comes to rest next to a plastic palm tree that has been placed in the bowl for some extra visual entertainment. B. Lynn empathizes with the crab. It seems bored and depressed.

***

B. Lynn is a lusty smoker; she loves smoking. It adds a little exciting tension to her life—like hanging out with a dangerous friend. Also, she has an obligation to continue a long-standing family tradition. There is, however, one side effect of smoking she finds offensive: the company of other smokers.

Since it's been determined cigarette smoke will kill anyone within a square mile of a smoker, she spends a lot of time hunched outside and forced into some kind of camaraderie with people she'd rather not talk to. She believes other smokers are ignorant because they are smoking.

As she sneaks out the back door to enjoy a cigarette without being exposed to anyone else's second-hand smoke, she feels Uncle Boy's shadow shivering her spine; he has decided they will be smoking comrades. Uncle Boy says, *So you're Snoot's daughter.*

B. Lynn glances at him and says, "Yep."

I met Snoot once. You're an awful lot like her.

Studying her hands, B. Lynn replies, "Yep." Searching for a topic that might lead them away from a discussion of her character flaws, B. Lynn roves her eyes around the backyard. Artfully placed in various locations are a little sign that says Grandma's Garden, a wooden cut-out of a fat lady bending over with her polka-dotted under-panted rear-end stuck in the air, and a plastic goose. Her eyes bounce off an automobile tire filled with dirt and dispirited vegetation, and then land on a tree stump the size of the Starship Enterprise. "That must have been a mighty big tree that came down," she says.

Nah–there weren't never no tree there. I dug that stump out of my buddy's yard, then me and some more of my buddies got a flat bed, rolled it onto the truck–it took six of us–and brought it over here. I thought it would make a nice decoration for the yard.

They sit in contemplative smoking camaraderie until the sky begins to weep. B. Lynn slogs back into the house carrying the awful weight of the tree stump in her head

Ancient Auntie is in the middle of her story about seeing Granddad Elrod standing in the hallway the night after he died. Soozie-Bells has her mouth scooched to one side, indicating she believes Ancient Auntie is not only a liar, she is senile— until B. Lynn reminds her that their mother saw dead Granddad Elrod standing in that very same hallway a couple of months after he shot himself in the head.

Aunt Larlene heaves herself out of her La-Z-Boy and says, *I have to go to the drugstore to get Sister some more suppositories and then I'm going to get us some of that KFC for supper. B. Lynn I want you to come with me. Susan Elizabeth, I want you stay here and talk to Sister.* B. Lynn is instantly a twelve-year-old on high alert for trouble and her mouth dries up like an old loofah sponge: her mother's voice is leaking out of Aunt Larlene's mouth. When they were kids, Susan Elizabeth was her sister's Going-to-Catch- Hell name and that hell quite often dribbled down onto B. Lynn.

It occurs to her that her sister will be left alone with Ancient Auntie, who is likely to take advantage of her weak personality and stuff her head full of messy family matters. In turn, Soozie-Bells will blow all that matter into B. Lynn's ears and B. Lynn feels she already has enough garbage rotting in her head. She suggests it might make for some extra fun if Soozie-Bells came along to the drugstore, but Aunt Larlene says *No—just you. And go pee before we leave.*

B. Lynn hustles down the dark hallway of spectral sightings, skittish that she might run into Granddad Elrod. Closing the bathroom door she immediately slams herself backward into some fusty towels hanging on a hook, and her right kidney takes a hit from the doorknob: body parts are dangling from the shower curtain rod.

Thinking of Ed Gein–the guy in the 1950s who cut people up and then used their skin to fashion lamp shades and other household items—she panics and grapples for the light switch; the fluorescence hums and flickers images of desiccated legs hung out for curing. When the tube light finally freezes on, she is relieved they are nothing more than Ancient Auntie's support stockings and a fleshy girdle—although they don't disturb any less than the thought of leg skin lamp shades.

She eases past the lifeless hosiery and contemplates the closed-mouth toilet. As she is nudging the lid open with her foot, her eyes grab onto a stack of reading material conveniently placed on the back of the toilet. Startled, she quickly retracts her foot: she hadn't expected that literature, albeit bathroom literature, would be any more available in Aunt Larlene's house than a water glass without residual crud. Grabbing a gummy copy of the 'Reader's Digest' from the top of the pile, she turns and plunks down on the toilet lid to read about what's going on in the world.

Aunt Larlene pounds on the bathroom door and yells, *What are you doing in there?*

B. Lynn yells, "What the heck do you think I'm doing?"

Aunt Larlene yells, *Well if you're having trouble going number two Sister has one suppository left in the medicine cabinet. Seeing as how we're going to the drugstore to get a new supply you can go ahead and use it if you need to. How much longer you going to be in there?*

Flipping through the remaining pages of 'BURIED ALIVE!'—B. Lynn yells, "About ten more minutes." *There's some Fleet enemas in the cupboard too.* When Aunt Larlene and B. Lynn return from the drugstore, Ancient Auntie is snoring into her bosom and Soozie-Bells is sitting erect and motionless. B. Lynn snaps her fingers in front of her glazed eyes; Soozie-Bells doesn't blink, but family matters are dribbling from her ears.

***

Mewing and purring, Aunt Larlene pads B. Lynn and Soozie-Bells up groaning stairs to her daughter, Irma Mae's, old bedroom; the fussing and fancying of the room in preparation for company has stirred Aunt Larlene's nesting instincts. B. Lynn, sensing her yearning mother cat-ishness, hopes she doesn't think they're going to be doing any suckling.

Aunt Larlene flings open her bedroom door with the flamboyance of a game show host revealing the prize behind door number three. Believing she might be time traveling, B. Lynn spins a look at Soozie-Bells to see if she's wearing a poodle skirt and saddle shoes: Irma Mae's bedroom is a carefully preserved testament to the life of a teenaged girl in the nineteen-fifties.

The pink chenille bedspread is burdened with stuffed bears and vacuous-faced dolls, nestled in autograph pillows penned with encouraging messages such as *Yours 'till Niagara Falls* and *To Irma Mae: I will always remember you. Love, Tammi."* Faded pennants—*Corn Valley High School* and *Go Cobbies Go!*—compete for wall space with framed black and white photographs of Hollywood icons dead for decades. B.   Lynn eyes the double bed. She's pretty sure they've become the equivalent of single beds since there are so many fat people around these days. She asks her sister where she plans on spending the night, because Soozie-Bells is not on her list of People She Will Sleep With. Soozie-Bells says, *Right next to you in that bed.*

"Like hell you are," B. Lynn replies. At the moment, she is despising Soozie-Bells with all the vehemence reserved for sisters; she is loathing the very sight of her. Soozie-Bells had visited Aunt Larlene, Uncle Boy, and Ancient Auntie last summer, and all she ever said about the experience was their house was weird and uncomfortable. B. Lynn always feels weird and uncomfortable so she didn't think that would be a problem. But she now realizes she has been thoroughly tricked into coming along on this trip because Soozie-Bells withheld some important information. She never mentioned that Aunt Larlene, Uncle Boy, and Ancient Auntie live in a little house of hoarders when she knew very well their decorative chaos would create schematic chaos in B. Lynn's brain. Aunt Larlene points to a chair dressed in clear plastic and tells them it is a reclining chair—a Perfect for Sleeping Chair. B. Lynn turns to Soozie-Bells and says, "Well! There you go!"

After a lingering satisfied look around the bedroom, Aunt Larlene claps her hands a couple of times and says, *I'll leave you two girls alone now so you can settle yourselves in and get comfy you let me know if there's anything else you all need.* B. Lynn can't imagine anything else they might need: the night stands and dressers have the landscape of a county dump. If they want a pink sock, some fuzzy LifeSavers, spent tissues, or a glass hazed white from the evaporation—they're all right there nice and handy.

"How long has it been since Irma Mae moved out of here?"

I don't know, Soozie-Bells says. *Maybe ten years.*

B. Lynn eyes the wadded tissues and speculates about whether they're dry with desiccated snot or wet with fresh snot.

"Do you suppose Uncle Boy comes in here to blow his nose?" *I don't know the first thing about what Uncle Boy does with his nose,* Soozie-Bells says. B. Lynn hesitates and then snatches a teddy bear off the bed. She implements its leg as a maneuvering device and edges the tissues off the dresser and onto the floor.

Gathering Irma Mae's dolls into her arms, B. Lynn thinks about what could happen if she yanked off their heads and tucked them into Aunt Larlene's and Uncle Boy's bed. It might make a fun surprise for them to discover decapitated dolls whispering under their blankets. Lost in a reverie of guillotining, she slowly becomes aware that something is murmuring, *Mama:* Tiny Tears is aggressively nuzzling her left breast. Digging her fingers into Tiny's frizzly hair, she flings her against the wall and then rapidly scrubs her hands up and down her pants. Soozie-Bells is busy rooting through the mess on her Perfect for Sleeping Chair. Mostly there are just a lot of crocheted afghans–the kind that are stitched in zigzag patterns and usually involve the colors orange and brown. She dumps them onto the pile of dolls and teddy bears, and she's feeling pretty happy with her job, until she discovers a pair of nylon panties giggling under a water-proof sitting pad. Pulling them out with the tips of her fingers, she holds them aloft like a big pink deflated balloon.

That night in bed, B. Lynn lies rigidly on her back staring at the ceiling and worrying about the cleanliness of her pillowcase. She rolls onto her side and peers at her sister slumped a few inches from her face, nicely tucked-up in her chair, and says, "Sweet Jesus, it's hot in here."

Soozie-Bells hisses, *At least you're not sitting in this damned Perfect for Sleeping Chair where Irma Mae used to stash her dirty underpants.*

***

Something God-Awful tries to kill Soozie-Bells in the middle of the night. It attacks her intestines first, roiling like a funky black cloud that bursts into a thunderstorm. It rushes to her stomach causing a torrential flow from her mouth that gives Niagara Falls stiff competition as one of the natural wonders of North America. Dashing between the bedroom and bathroom, she calls on the Father, Son, and her Ex-Husband: *Good God– Jesus Christ–Son of a BITCH—* and B. Lynn believes she is the most grievously inconvenient sister she has ever known. The next morning, B. Lynn feels pretty dragged-down and fed-up— what with Soozie-Bells knocking into her bed and behaving in a generally obnoxious manner all night. She is also suffering the effects of oxygen deprivation, having had to lie face-down in her bed and breathe through her arm skin in case Soozie-Bells was leaving a miasma of contagion in her wake. If her sister has a chance to pass on something nasty to her, she'll do it. Soozie-Bells lives alone so she doesn't understand the concept of consideration; she has probably touched every single thing in their bedroom and bathroom with her Something God-Awful infested hands and has likely breathed all over the place, too. B. Lynn is disheartened by the prospect of sharing what has become her sister's favorite room, and in order to minimize the surface space for germs to stick onto the bottoms of her feet, she stumps to the bathroom on her heels.

Aunt Larlene, Uncle Boy, and Ancient Auntie are slopped in the living watching 'Sponge Bob Square Pants.' The three of them are fixated on the television with the same bright-eyed, crazed intensity of sight hounds tracking a rabbit. B. Lynn crawls into her sitting hole and tries to dredge all thoughts about everything out of her head. When Aunt Larlene notices her hiding in her hole, she grabs the remote and shoots Sponge Bob through the heart so she and Uncle Boy can hash out detailed accounts of all the times they have been sicker than Soozie-Bells. When they tire of waxing nostalgic about their illnesses, the conversation turns to a discussion of Soozie-Bell's blood sugar levels.

Uncle Boy pontificates on the hazards of diabetes and muses about which of the negatives effects of the disease will likely kill Soozie-Bells. She has had Type I Diabetes since she was twelve-years-old so he figures she will go blind or have her feet lopped off any day now. Before he retired Uncle Boy was a nurses' aide which is almost like being a doctor. As they are easily attained from her sitting hole, B. Lynn gobbles Brown 'N Serve rolls all morning—Ancient Auntie whips up a batch every few hours and then sets them around the house for convenient snacking. By lunchtime B. Lynn is uncomfortably bloated from her breakfast Brown 'N Serve binge; she decides to eat a reasonable lunch so she will lose a few pounds by dinnertime.

In the refrigerator she discovers numerous bowls covered with waxed paper secured with rubber bands, crimped bundles of tin foil in a variety of sizes and condition, and an assortment of weeping jars and bottles. There is an abundance of leftover KFC coleslaw—B. Lynn doesn't like to fill up on cabbage and shaved carrots when there is grease and breading available— and apparently Aunt Larlene and Uncle Boy have the same policy: they left that slaw alone and let Soozie-Bells and Ancient Auntie feel self-righteous about sitting up at the table eating their vegetables.

Because it is the only food she can identify, she snags the plastic container of coleslaw and squeaks off the lid. Nestled in the cabbage drowning in Miracle Whip is a cunning little vegetative creature blooming in soft shades of lavender and blue. Its furry little face peeks up at B. Lynn and she yells, "I found the Something God-Awful."

***

In case B. Lynn and Soozie-Bells proved to be boring, Aunt Larlene had also lured her daughter, Irma Mae, and Irma Mae's third wife, Patty, to stay for the week as backup fun. They grind into the driveway around two o'clock that afternoon, their car fuming smoke and squalling about the flat-bed trailer ungraciously hooked onto its rear-end. At first, B. Lynn thinks they might have brought their own stove and refrigerator—the way some people have to take their pillows wherever they go—but snarling under the bondage of clothes-line and duct tape are two dreadful black wheel chairs. She doesn't remember Aunt Larlene mentioning that Irma Mae and Patty are crippled, so she asks, "Are Cousin Irma Mae and Third-Wife-Patty crippled?"

They think they are, Aunt Larlene replies.

Getting their car and flat-bed situated in the short driveway with an incline like the up side of a teeter-totter, affords Aunt Larlene and Uncle Boy the opportunity for the shouting out of directions and waving about of their arms. This task makes them feel important and also it is something to do for a few minutes.

Ancient Auntie, wanting a piece of the importance for herself, clutches the porch railing with her bird-feet hands and screeches at B. Lynn to help Irma Mae out of the car. B. Lynn glances at Uncle Boy and then squats down and fiddles with the laces on her sneakers to give him time to get to the car first. Since he was a nurses' aide B. Lynn figures he must be used to hauling people around and also she just had a flash image of an Irma Mae without legs. The thought of lugging her torso across the yard makes her sick to her stomach.

Before Uncle Boy can lumber over to the car, Irma Mae and Patty spring out the doors of their car like a couple of jack-in-the-box clowns, so startling to B. Lynn she tips over backwards in her squat position. Patty bounces across the driveway and yanks her to her feet. B. Lynn's spine voices severe objections about the rapid straightening from a tipped-over squat, so she calls dibs on one of the wheelchairs and wants to know why the heck they have them in the first place. Irma Mae claims her arches are likely to collapse at any time so she is reluctant to use her feet. Patty suffers with a twitching condition that makes walking a hazardous activity. They brought the wheelchairs in case they decide to go to Wal-Mart.

Uncle Boy herds everyone to the basement—he is in a dither because he has a present for Irma Mae and Patty. Flipping on the lights, he then pats his hands together and rocks on his heels for the happiness of his surprise: moldering in a corner is a bed of great expanse and height; a bed slumped, depressed, and broken-backed.

I thought you gals would appreciate a bed where you could spread yourselves out in. I got me a deal at the Salvation Army—this here's a king-size and they wanted twelve bucks for it but I chewed them down to ten. B. Lynn thinks to tell Soozie-Bells she should be damned grateful for her Perfect for Sleeping Chair.

The basement is quite extensive, given the size of the house, and B. Lynn can't tell if she's experiencing one of those fun-house optical illusions or if Uncle Boy tunneled around to make some extra space. She wanders off to look for signs of excavation and discovers a closed door. She jiggles the knob but the door stands its ground. She asks what's in there and Uncle Boy says, *Ray.*

"Ray? Who the hell is RAY?"

He's the man who rents that room.

"Well—is he in there now?"

I don't know where he is he's a grown man and can come and go as he pleases, Uncle Boy replies. B. Lynn hasn't noticed a bathroom in that basement so she is troubled about where, exactly, Ray comes and goes.

***

Uncle Boy has, at his fingertips, his greatest achievement. After years of careful and patient nurturing, he has grown his fingernails to such an excessive length that his hands are worthy of display in a side show at the county fair. They weigh down his fingers and inhibit any delicate work such as turning the pages of a book, or buttoning his shirt to conceal the few hairs that sprout unhappily on his sunken chest.

B. Lynn's mother had long fingernails, filed to a point and painted red; they were perfect people-poking weapons. But Uncle Boy's are of a different nature. His nails are talons, hawk-ish and anciently yellow. Slightly curved under at the tips, they are rendered useless for poking—although he could use them to nudge. Each nail is imbedded with black matter, particles of debris bearing testimony to his various activities over the past couple years.

If Uncle Boy died of unusual circumstances a medical examiner might scrape out the refuse from one nail, examine it, and conclude: *Here is a bit of grease from changing the oil in the car, here is evidence that he handled fried chicken; there is an indication that he dug diligently at a mosquito bite.*

To impress upon them that he isn't just another decaying body cluttering up the house, Uncle Boy offers to make hamburgers for supper. Baffled by the complexities of preparing solid meat, B. Lynn has become a culinary artist of ground meat and so she is eager to observe and correct Uncle Boy's technique in the handling of their hamburgers. But as she watches him dig his fingers into the raw meat, molding and pummeling it into patties, her esophagus quivers. When her stomach sees little worms of pink flesh dangle moistly from beneath his fingernails it shrieks: *Don't even THINK about sending an Uncle Boy burger down here.*

When he has a platter fully populated with hamburgers that bear a strong resemblance to deformed fetal pigs, Uncle Boy takes it to the grill in the backyard, so riddled with rust B. Lynn tries to remember when she last had a tetanus shot. He lightly warms the burgers over lighter fluid smoke and then slaps them back onto the platter so they might marinate for a moment in their own blood. Holding the platter aloft like a priest celebrating the Holy Eucharist, he returns to the house and bangs it onto the kitchen table. He yells, *Everybody get in here and eat.*

Uncle Boy looks at B. Lynn with eager expectation as she hazards the first bite of her hamburger. With the warmed meat squatting stolidly on her tongue, her throat muscles become paralyzed and refuse to accept the delivery of food. She realizes the burger is contaminating her tongue, more vulnerable than her teeth, so she works her mouth around until she gets it lodged in her cheek. With her first mouthful safely packed away her throat is willing to perform an empty swallow; she wonders how much more of her dinner she can stuff in her cheeks before she looks like she's storing nuts for winter.

B. Lynn slides her eyes at Patty sitting across the table next to Uncle Boy. Hunched and looking defeated, she is clutching her hamburger in her left hand, hovering it over her plate as if she doesn't have the strength to lift her hand to her mouth.

Uncle Boy is bold with his bodily emissions: he holds to the school of thought that withholding gaseous disturbances in his stomach and intestines is detrimental to his health.

Stretching wide his mouth, he releases a belligerent disturbance. He leans sideways in his chair and releases another.

Patty drops her hamburger onto her plate of baked beans and potato salad and looks at B. Lynn. Her shoulders are bobbing up and down as if they are attached to strings controlled by an invisible puppet master, and with each jerk a tear spills from her eyes. Watching Patty, B. Lynn blinks hard and fast to inhibit her own spillage, but her shoulders are out of control and convulsing with suppressed emotion. B. Lynn doesn't know if she and Patty are laughing or crying.

***

After dinner Aunt Larlene announces, *It's time for me and Sister's shows so let's everybody sit down and watch some TV—Boy you go pack your bags and vamoose.* B. Lynn can't figure why Uncle Boy is the only one getting permission to vamoose and she would like to know what he did to instigate the vamoosing so she might use it for future reference.

"What did he do?" B. Lynn says.

What do you mean 'what did he do,' Aunt Larlene replies. *What does he ever do.*

"Then what has he done?"

He's never done a darned thing to my knowledge.

"Well," B. Lynn says. "I'd like to know why you're letting him vamoose"

Because we're going to have us a little quality girl time without some man slobbering around the house that's why.

***

Caterwauling like cows at milking time, Aunt Larlene, Ancient Auntie and Irma Mae, shout out so many right answers during 'Wheel of Fortune' B. Lynn figures it's a rerun.

Becoming suffused with the excitement and heat of competition she eventually joins in with the caterwauling, but she doesn't know any right answers and neither does Patty. She wishes they were watching 'Hoarders' so she could explain the concept to them. Then they watch 'The Biggest Loser,' which makes everyone quiet. B. Lynn glances around at all the expansive flesh right there in Ancient Auntie's living room and thinks they could probably start their own show. It is the beginning of the season so all the Losers are in full bloom. Their bellies look familiar so B. Lynn palpates her own for comparison, and she never should have done that because it was depressing.

***

The next morning, B. Lynn lists down the stairs to the living room and discovers Irma Mae and Patty slumped on the sofa with what might have been dead Granddad Elrod's blankets tucked under their first chins. Patty is twitching, which jiggles Irma Mae, which gives both of them the appearance of having springs for necks like a couple of dime store bobble heads. All they need are some plastic eyeballs rolling in their sockets and they'd be ready to put on the shelf.

Aunt Larlene's recliner is yawning wide and empty and there are only a few dusty feathers floating around Ancient Auntie's vacant perch. When she asks Irma Mae and Patty if they vamoosed, Irma Mae sucks all the air out of the room and Patty's lips disappear into her mouth like a couple of night crawlers slipping into their worm holes.

They study her intently, without the least bit of friendliness, for such a great length of time that B. Lynn begins to feel she might be responsible for the whereabouts of Ancient Auntie and Aunt Larlene. She hopes she didn't get up in the middle of the night and accidently kill them.

Patty finally unfurls her lips and says, *Didn't you hear all the commotion right outside your bedroom last night?* B. Lynn isn't sure she should answer any questions without having her lawyer present, but she shakes her head no, no she didn't hear a thing. She figures if she doesn't say anything out loud they won't be able to pin something on her.

Irma Mae says, *Well your Ancient Auntie is in the hospital. The Something God-Awful got at her in the middle of the night.* B. Lynn is sad about Ancient Auntie: if she dies they might have to extend their visit because they'll have to go to the funeral.

"What do you suppose the odds are that the Something God-Awful will kill her?" B. Lynn asks.

Patty contemplates the possibility and decides they should write a eulogy for Ancient Auntie right now—it will be one less thing to worry about if they have to go shopping for new funeral clothes and order cakes and punch for a reception they could have afterwards. She seems pretty keen on the idea. She says, *She was a fine strong woman.*

Irma Mae sighs, *The last of the Merckle kids. Now they'll all be together in heaven.* That statement causes B. Lynn a painful episode of the nose and throat snortle-choke because she has grave doubts any of the Merckle's are in heaven.

Reluctant to let Irma Mae and Patty get all the credit for the saying of nice things, B. Lynn adds, "She took really good care of her wigs, too." She gazes at Ancient Auntie's shady corner of the living room and tries to imagine her languorously waving her wings as she plucks a harp. But all she can see is Ancient Auntie crouched on her chair, using her walker to push at the flames as her pigeon feathers pop and sizzle.

Patty, squirming deeper into what might have been dead Granddad Elrod's blanket, says *She'll be with your Granddad Elrod, too.* B. Lynn is still troubled about the usage history of those blankets and wonders if there's still some Granddad Elrod left on them—maybe some tiny hairs that got woven into the fibers. She thinks about DNA. She has never personally seen any DNA—she thinks it might be like dandruff, little bits of flaky skin—but she's watched enough episodes of CSI to know they scrape it off dead people.

She realizes Ancient Auntie might have tracked Granddad Elrod's DNA all over the house after he died and that there could still be some settled in the carpet along with the Dorito crumbs and Uncle Boy's toenail clippings. She hopes Aunt Larlene doesn't come home littered with the stuff. Sometimes the CSI agents take DNA from people who knew the dead person—maybe someone will be coming to the house to scrape their tongues.

Thinking about tongues alerts B. Lynn's taste buds; she wanders into the kitchen to find something that will make them happy. As she is poking around in the refrigerator crammed with items of dubious provenance and identity, she spots a biscuit wedged between the stove and kitchen counter. Grabbing a spatula, she levers it free of its entrapment and then runs her forefinger along the edge of the counter to gather crumbly biscuit excavation debris. She sticks her finger in her mouth and her tongue is pleased with the results of her foraging—after tussling with an Uncle Boy burger, it has become very complacent about what it will accept.

Irma Mae and Patty have unearthed a paper plate from under the sofa cushions and they're using it to write down a list of Ancient Auntie's finer qualities. Every few seconds, Irma Mae digs the pen back and forth on the paper plate where the ink keeps sliding over the greasy spots.

When B. Lynn leans over to see what kinds of lies they are telling, biscuit crumbs dance onto the paper plate; Irma Mae grinds the pen to a stop and Patty stares at the crumbs as if they are driplets of spittle. The air clogs with their contempt of B. Lynn's biscuit and she doesn't know if that's because it is considered ungracious to eat while preparing a memorial service, or because they know where it came from.

Soozie-Bells finally slumps into the living room and right away Irma Mae and Patty ask if she slept okay and how is she feeling and so on. Everyone is under the impression that because she has diabetes she is a lot more fragile and needy than B. Lynn, which is annoying because she has the constitution of an old war horse and B. Lynn quite often feels ill and receives little attention.

Irma Mae and Patty are busy pawing at Soozie-Bells to make her more comfortable, when the front door slams open and Aunt Larlene bulls into the house, squinting and sniffing around the living room as if she thinks everyone might have been having some fun while she was gone.

Her suspicious attitude causes Irma Mae's throat to make short revving sounds like a beat car on a frigid morning because Aunt Larlene has corrupted genes; genes that have traveled down through generations of Merckles like the roots of a noxious plant.

These genes have given them the ability to make the innocent believe they are guilty of detestable behavior when, in fact, they had been doing nothing more than sitting in a corner minding their own business. The weak-natured are left with varying side effects from the Merckle guilt poison: some suffer with Post Traumatic Stress Syndrome, causing them to have flashbacks of absolutely nothing; others become Alzheimer's hypochondriacs, constantly worrying about the health of their minds because they come to believe they were indeed guilty of detestable behavior and they can't remember what it was.

Irma Mae eases sideways and shuffles the paper plate under her posterior sponginess. B. Lynn hopes that if the Something

God-Awful sucks the last of the stale air out of Ancient Auntie's lungs, she'll take the time to copy the eulogy down on a nice piece of stationary rather than reading it from a paper plate she's pulled out of her rear end.

Aunt Larlene yells, *You all go put some clothes on,* but it isn't understood if they're supposed to get dressed because she thinks they are a slovenly mess or if Ancient Auntie is dead and they have to go look at her body. Then she yells, *And somebody pack themselves some toiletries—I don't care who. I need some rest and Sister can't stay alone tonight.*

Right away Irma Mae squeezes and kneads her feet as if she's getting two slabs of white bread dough ready to pop in the oven, and Patty does some exploratory moaning and twitching. Soozie-Bells is inch-worming her index finger up her chin toward her mouth and it occurs to B. Lynn that she is going to sneak her finger down her throat so she will throw up again, giving her a good excuse to go back to her Perfect for Sleeping Chair.

B. Lynn yells, "Cut it out." Because her voice sounds a lot like their mother's, Soozie-Bells has a memory flood and quickly regresses to childhood behavior: she bunches up and squeezes her eyes shut, believing she has made herself invisible.

Aunt Larlene still hasn't given any useful information about the exact state of Ancient Auntie's body so it isn't clear if she can't be left alone while she is laid out in a hospital bed half-dead, or if someone has to hold vigil while she's laid out on a mortuary slab completely dead.

B. Lynn asks, "Where are we going?"

THE HOSPITAL, Aunt Larlene shouts.

Relief washes over B. Lynn like a warm shower because she doesn't go to hospitals. "I don't go to hospitals," she says.

175

You are so going to the hospital it might be the one last time you'll ever see your Ancient Auntie alive.

Seeing Ancient Auntie alive one last time has never been an item on B. Lynn's bucket list. She slides her eyes toward Soozie-Bells to gauge her desire to be involved in the ugly business. But Soozie-Bells has bunched up and squeezed her eyes shut again so no one can see her.

***

Irma Mae, Patty, B. Lynn and Soozie-Bells, cluster in the doorway of Ancient Auntie's hospital room like a bunch of rubes at a sideshow. They stare at the desolate landscape of blankets and sheets on a bed that appears to be Ancient Auntie-less. The Merckles wear spitefulness like skunks wear stripes so it is very likely Aunt Larlene tricked them into coming to the hospital when she knew darned well Ancient Auntie was already dead.

B. Lynn feels sorry that Ancient Auntie might be dead. She had stopped in the gift shop to buy her a present and now she's probably stuck with the damned thing. She wonders if she can take it back or if they have a rule about not accepting returns once a present has been out of the shop and exposed to blood and urine and all the other stuff that slops around in hospitals.

She had picked out a white ceramic angel holding a little gold heart sign that reads: *May God Bless You and Keep You Safe*—it seemed the kind of thing that Ancient Auntie might enjoy taking home to put with her Jesus decorations. Patty thinks it is precious, so if the gift shop people say it's contaminated B. Lynn is pretty sure she can sell it to her and get back her four dollars and fifty-seven cents.

Crushed between Irma Mae and Patty, B. Lynn can feel little eruptions of goose pimples on their arms. She figures they're either exciting themselves about the nice memorial service they have planned or they're thinking about a visit to the morgue. When Irma Mae starts picking at the things B. Lynn nudges forward into Soozie-Bells' back because she doesn't know if goose pimples pop like face pimples. Sifting through her knowledge of pricky skin conditions she concludes there must be more than one pimple species, as she doesn't recall ever getting the goose kind on her chin.

The bed sheets begin snaking around and B. Lynn says, "What the hell is that."

Patty says, *Go look.*

"You go look," B. Lynn replies, and Soozie-Bells looks at the floor.

Irma Mae says, *I'll go look*—and she is exactly the right person to explore the peculiar business going on under the sheets. She had a heart attack a few years ago, and the rest of them are still in relatively good health. It wouldn't make good sense for anyone else to risk damaging their hearts when hers is already wrecked. Also, as Ancient Auntie's eldest niece, Irma Mae stands to inherit her walker and chair.

As soon as Irma Mae touches the sheet it is too hard for B. Lynn not to yell, 'squirrel!' so she yells "SQUIRREL!" Soozie-Bells shrieks and then B. Lynn shrieks because there really might be a squirrel snuffling around for a stray canned pea or maybe a flake of DNA.

Patty starts in with her twitching and moaning so that she looks as if she needs a quick-fix exorcism. B. Lynn yanks her hair and tells her if a nurse catches her acting like that she'll probably get hauled away so someone can inspect the inside of her head. She tells her if Ancient Auntie is dead they might be able to leave the hospital right away—but if she has to have a Cat-Scan, the rest of them are going to be stuck hanging around for days because doctors like to give people plenty of opportunities to die so they won't have to waste their time reading the test results. Irma Mae yells, *It's Ancient Auntie for crying out loud you all get in here.*

Before entering the room, B. Lynn pumps-out some hand sanitizer from one of those dispensers that hang on the wall and smears it under her nose to act as a barricade against germs that might try to crawl into her nostrils. She instantly feels as if she has a brush fire mustache and Patty tells her of course it burns because hand sanitizer is mostly alcohol. B. Lynn wonders if she can drink it.

The closer to Ancient Auntie's bed, the more objectionable the air. B. Lynn says, "Christ it stinks in here."

Soozie-Bells says, *Breathe through your mouth*—but B. Lynn will never breathe through her mouth and she doesn't understand people who do. If you breathe through your mouth the stink will glom onto your tastes buds so whenever you eat something that stink will get all mixed in with your food. She asks Soozie-Bells if she thinks it would be an enjoyable experience to eat a bologna sandwich with that stink-taste in her mouth.

Edging to the side of the bed B. Lynn looks down at Ancient Auntie blinking up at her like a broken baby bird. She looks down and sees her mother and grandparents and their parents. She looks down and sees her children and grandchildren and their children.

Ancient Auntie clutches B. Lynn's arm and says, *It's been so nice having you come visit. I hope you all had some fun.*

B. Lynn pats her hand and says, "We had a wonderful time. We had an absolutely wonderful time."

Trashed

B. Lynn, traveling with her daughter, Wumpo, her son-in-law, Medium A, and her three grandchildren, believes they should become familiar with the languages and customs of the regions they are visiting. It will be an enriching experience for the grandkids, Geigers, the J-Man and Pie, to learn about other cultures and also, when she surprises them with her expansive knowledge of the world, she's pretty sure it will guarantee an invitation to join them on their next vacation.

Parked in front of a Red Roof Inn in West Virginia, she conducts a rehearsal of the words and phrases that might best demonstrate that they are not ignorant—indeed, they are very well-informed: *We bin travelin since yesterday night! Git! We done did that! Egg-suckin dog!*

In the event her grandkids are exposed to some West Virginian-Americans, she cautions them against using the term 'hillbilly.' A stunned silence settles in the van, the grandkids with their mouths hanging open like three dead guppies. Wumpo snaps, *I can't believe you just said the H-word in front of the kids, MOM. Jesus.*

B. Lynn and Medium A make the determination to leave Wumpo and the kids slopping in the van while they go into the motel to inquire about rooms, because the kids won't hardly shut-up—and Wumpo deserves to be shut up with them.

Denying the existence of her children, snarling and foaming in their car seats like caged Pit Bull puppies without distemper shots, Wumpo had spent the day lounging in the front seat drooling into her pillow, her legs stretched onto the dash board. So that she might further simulate the comforts of a La-Z-Boy, she had ratcheted down the back of her seat until it was lying in B. Lynn's lap, which might have provided her with a nice little table for snacks except she didn't want Wumpo's oral leakage getting her Cheese Doodles soggy.

B. Lynn had warned her if the airbag decided to make an unexpected appearance and explode out of the dashboard, her legs would be flung straight up into the air and her knee caps would be firmly embedded in her eye sockets. She would spend the rest of her life looking like a bobby pin and it would make walking damned near impossible. Wumpo hadn't minded about that. B. Lynn had told her if one of her legs snapped off it could sail right in her direction, possibly delivering a fatal blow to her head which would create one hell of a disturbing vacation memory for the kids—seeing their grandmother being dead in the back seat. She hadn't minded about that, either.

Un-mucking themselves from the kid slurry in the van, Medium A practices walking staggery-like in the parking lot and B. Lynn removes her dental plate so people will know they know where they are.

Haggard-gaiting like a couple of zombies fresh from their graves, Medium A and B. Lynn enter the motel lobby which looks like the interior of an orange crate with a coffee pot. Banging her hand on the counter, B. Lynn announces, "We done come a fur piece!"

The concierge replies, *Pleese, you buy fur peecis down te rood.*

B. Lynn shoots her eyes at Medium A. The emerging moonscape on his head makes him very sensitive about any discussion of fur pieces. But he only twitches a touch and says, *We are awontin summa yurn rooms to let. We got us a messa caterwaulin tuckered yougins needin some warshin an sleepin. Thays three ovum plus my woman waitin in my ve-hicle an thays all ahungrin and thurstin so mebbe you might point us'ins in the deerekshun of a fine restrunt, too.*

The concierge says, *Pleese, no allow messa caterwallins—you go up te rood for tat kind of bissiniss.*

B. Lynn looks at Medium A and says, "He ain't unnerstandin' nuthin' we got to say an I ain't unnerstandin' nuthin' what he got to say, neither."

She realizes they are culture shocking each other and wishes she had thought to pack a burqa. It is uncomfortable having the concierge look at her naked in her clothes so she snags a copy of the Al Jazeera Times, tucking it under her chin so that it will hang down to conceal a portion of her offensive parts, and then shields her face with a greasy issue of The National Enquirer.

Just as B. Lynn is thinking to fetch her granddaughter, Pie, because she is the loudest talker of her loud-talking grandchildren and loud talking often assists in the comprehension of foreign languages, Medium A displays the palm of his left hand and makes scribbling motions with his right hand. The concierge's blank window-shade face snaps open because he no longer din't unnerstand what Medium A is sayin'.

Whining a hum with the pitch of a mosquito scouting for blood—or maybe a sitar—the concierge drops from view behind the counter. After a moment of rustling and thunking, he pops up waving a scrap of paper over his head, his mouth stretched into a gold nugget grin. B. Lynn wonders if he invests in gold teeth rather than keeping a savings account.

Pumping his eyebrows up and down so he looks as though he has two furry caterpillars doing push-ups on his forehead, the concierge reverently places the scrap on the counter.

Medium A clamps onto a pencil and carefully draws two boxes: two beds in the first box and one bed in the second box. He adds five tiny lollypops in the box with two beds; a single lollipop in the box with one bed. B. Lynn thinks it is clever of

Medium A to request lollipops in the rooms rather than chocolates—which offer only a fleeting pleasure, whereas lollipops can last more than an hour if you refrain from vigorous sucking.

Tugging on Medium A's arm to bring his head closer to hers, she points at the picture and says, "We can suck all night!"

Medium A tears his arm from her grasp, finding the proximity of her head unappealing, and says, *Those are supposed to be people, B. LYNN,* and she doesn't like his snotty tone when he said, *Those are supposed to be people, B. LYNN.* Mothers-in-law have bad reputations so he had preconceived notions about her when he married Wumpo, tending to get bristly even though she always speaks kindly when advising him about the right way to do things.

Glancing back at the picture she now clearly sees those suckers do indeed look just like the little pink and blue people in the 'Life' game. One of the people has a squiggly body like a representation of a sperm and she hopes Medium A and the concierge won't take notice, because it would be embarrassing to be in the same room with two men looking at a sperm.

It occurs to B. Lynn that she doesn't like her son-in-law and she doesn't want to see any more of his dirty pictures. She turns away and idles her mind around the word 'concierge.' Concierge gives the impression of a motel with more than one floor and maybe some cookies in the lobby, and she wonders if it is merely a fancy word for receptionist—although receptionist sounds as if the person doing the recepting is a female. She thinks there might be a masculine form of the word such as recreceptionater or receptionmentor. Barista also sounds girly so maybe barista boys are called baristos.

Returning to the van, B. Lynn boings her head into Wumpo's open window to cause her alarm and also to ask about the correct gender usages of receptionist and barista. Wumpo doesn't respond to her question because she is engaged in thumb calisthenics on her phone and is thus completely unaware life on earth exists.

B. Lynn rummages in her purse for her own brain melting device and shoots her a message. Wumpo texts back: *They r called reception & coffee persons MOM. Jesus.*

***

B. Lynn decides to walk to her room because she is sick and tired of her kids and sick and tired of their kids, too. The motel runs as two rows of slumping barracks, gazing sullenly at each other across a parking lot that is so pieced and patched together it looks like a picture puzzle of Pompeii when it was covered with the drying vomit of Mount Vesuvius.

But it seems a quaint place, reminiscent of the old state route lodgings in which she, her parents and sister, had spent fitful nights while on her mother's determined vacations to visit her howling mess of a family in Arkansas. She is startled by the thought that she is now traveling with her own howling mess of a family, and all of them are swimming around in a treacherous and murky gene pool.

Scuffing along, troubled about the ancestry sludge that might have mucked down to her grandchildren, she becomes aware that there are lots of merry folks muddling around the open doors of their rooms.

They wave—a few salute—and it pleases her that they might think she is a soldier. As she is raising her hand to return the gestures of friendliness, a pricky prejudice jumps out of a dark recess in her head and skewers the unthinking part of her brain.

It is a curiosity, this pricky prejudice: she wasn't aware she had one in residence. This may be due, in part, because she has always lived in a village where there is nothing to be prejudiced about.

As she is examining her pricky prejudice for its type of pickiness, it begins rocking back and forth behind her eyeballs, screaming, *TAKE A LOOK AROUND US FOR CRYING OUT LOUD*—and she understands her pricky prejudice is entirely dependent upon locale.

B. Lynn loves merry folks in New Orleans. When she is in New Orleans it would seem a fine thing to be dandled upon the knees of the grandfathers hunkered on curbs, engaging in earnest conversations with their whiskey bottle friends, whom they have tenderly clothed in little brown paper jackets.

When merry folks in New Orleans congest the sidewalks, cooking up a messa sumpin' on their charcoal grills, she senses they are having a loving family reunion—without their relatives—and the possum smells good, too.

In New Orleans, if a bare-chested youth with hair ropes dangling from his head and a nose bone dripping from his septum, raises his beer bottle in greeting and good cheer, she feels he is a kindred spirit and wishes to know him better.

When folks weary of being merry in New Orleans they nestle in doorways and on stoops for a peaceful night's slumber and it is cozy and fun—like a big slumber party—and she yearns to tuck their plastic bags under their chins and give them a gentle kiss goodnight on their foreheads.

But when she is walking to her motel room in West Virginia, she finds merry folks involved in these same activities disturbing and she doesn't like them.

Because B. Lynn's children enjoy hearing her opinions and thoughts on various subjects, as soon as they pull into their parking space she scuttles to the van to share her pricky prejudice revelation.

Wumpo, quiet for a moment, says, *I can't believe you're a white trash profiler, MOM.*

The J-Man yells, *You're not supposed to dig around in other people's TRASH, BOBBA.*

***

Medium A un-bunches himself from the van and immediately begins grappling, in a sweaty snarly way, with B. Lynn's suitcase. She yells, "I'll get that."

Medium A yells, *Not a problem, B. LYNN.*

Geigers yells, *Remember about the dead people Daddy!*

The J-Man yells, *Oh my gosh Daddy don't let the dead people fall out of Bobba's suitcase—oh my GOSH Daddy!*

Pie and Wumpo don't yell anything because Pie is moaning and chewing the tail of her black rubber security rat and Wumpo is practicing invisibility.

So as not to be openly hostile, and never wanting to offend, Medium A quite often veils his displeasure of things by making little snide-lets. He believes this underhanded method of complaining gives the impression that he is a humorous fellow while still making it known that he is unhappy. His snide-lets also provide an escape route if anyone points out that he is not funny—he is plainly snotty—because he can say, *I was only KIDDING.*

And so, as he was loading the van for their trip, rather than saying, *Your suitcase is too damned heavy,* he said, *How many bodies do you have in here, B.Lynn.* Because of the hateful stories Wumpo has told her children about her, they were willing to believe she had, indeed, rolled up some stray corpses—perhaps tucking them in with her underpants—and that she might have left room for a few grandchildren. B. Lynn was not inclined to dissuade them of the notion because terrified children behave better.

In order to make the dragging of her suitcase across the parking lot a pleasant event for Medium A, she scurries to open the door of her room as a show of hospitality. Her key scitters around the keyhole in a palsied exhibit of nervousness and excitement: Medium A is stalking up behind her like a red-faced rooster ready for a cock fight and having a motel room all to herself is a luxury she has always longed to experience. She has stayed in plenty motels, but never when nothing was expected of her.

The key, becoming impatient with lock foreplay, abruptly thrusts itself into the hole and B. Lynn steps into her room, panting with the anticipation of not having to share the cunning little bottles of shampoo and conditioner; the small bars of real facial soap—and maybe a mint.

A visual and olfactory assault immediately activates her retching and crying reflexes. She decides to retch first and cry later, because doing both at the same time causes a great deal of discord between the nose and mouth. The mouth, being the first southern destination for anything that wants to escape the unfortunate living conditions in the nose, quite often finds the sudden influx of nose immigrants objectionable and it will stage a rebellion by throwing up.

Medium A, steadily pushing her suitcase against the backs of her legs in a way that could not be construed as blatant shoving, peers over her shoulder and remarks that she can pretend she is camping. She tells him camping involves clean dirt whereas her motel room involves filthy dirt. He merely shrugs, because he doesn't know dirt about dirt.

Noticing the chain lock dangly morosely from a single screw in shattered woodwork—a pretty good indication that someone was mighty determined to get in or mighty determined to get out—B. Lynn asks Medium A if she should be concerned that someone might try to get at her in the middle of the night. He says, *Well, shove you're ninety pound suitcase against the door—that should slow the stampede.* But she knows he is really saying, *You would be damned lucky if someone wanted to get at you in the middle of the night.*

***

Resembling blackened Fourth of July sparklers without the happiness, B. Lynn immediately knows them for what they are, and what they are—are witching wires. The dreadful objects protrude from various locations in her motel room woodwork, which is so splintered and hacked upon, B. Lynn wonders if Jack Torrance—*Honey? I'm home*—from the movie 'The Shining' has spent a restless night in her room.

Wumpo wants to know what makes her think they're witching wires—and what the heck are witching wires, anyway. B. Lynn says she doesn't know what the heck are witching wires—but if such a thing exists, those must be them—what else could they be. Wumpo thinks maybe they're cameras because she wouldn't know a witching wire if it poked her in the eye. B. Lynn tells her if some dismal soul takes a bit of pleasure from watching her sixty-two-year-old body slop around a motel room, they must have nothing lovely in their life and she would be happy to do them a kind service. But these are definitely witching wires—can she not feel their smoldering evilness?

Wumpo closes her eyes. After several moments, she begins swaying and buzzing a flat-line hum. At first, B. Lynn thinks it is the witching wires doing the buzzing humming—charging themselves up in preparation for springing out of the woodwork— but then it occurs to her that Wumpo might have fallen under a hideous witching wire spell.

The precise method for the un-casting of spells eludes her; she can't remember if she should stick Wumpo with a pin or kiss her on her lips. The only pin she has on hand is the safety pin she's using as a button for her pants; removing it would require intense and hazardous work, involving the squeezing in of her stomach and painful muscular contortions of her torso. There is also a chance the safety pin is perfectly happy right where it is—in which case, it might defend its position by inserting itself into her belly. And she isn't inclined to kiss Wumpo on her lips because she has drool paste in the corners of her mouth. B. Lynn decides slapping her face might be a viable option and it is also something she had been longing to do since the beginning of their trip.

Wumpo suddenly flips open her eyes and says she thinks she can—yes, she definitely can feel the smoldering evilness. B. Lynn wants to know if she had sensed possession, too—what with all her buzzing humming. Wumpo says she was buzzing and humming for a bit of entertainment. She says it was very boring standing around with nothing to do but wait for a sense of the smoldering evilness—tiring too—and B. Lynn feels her hand quiver with desire for slapping.

She asks Wumpo what she is going to do about the witching wire situation, and Wumpo says, *I don't see why I should have to do anything about it. They aren't my witching wires.* She folds her arms and lifts her chin in a mutinous way.

B. Lynn had seen enough of that kind of behavior when Wumpo was teenager, so she says, "I don't like your smart-alecky attitude one little bit Missy. Stand up straight and push the hair out of your eyes."

Everyone in the family calls upon Medium A when there is an unpleasant task to be done; he is their unpleasant task master, and the removal of witching wires seems like something he should be required to do. B. Lynn says, "Call Medium A."

Looking like a fawn paralyzed in her mother's headlights, Wumpo stands motionless for a moment and then snaps, *I'm not calling him,* which gives B. Lynn the understanding she would rather be in her mother's room dealing with witching wires, than be in her own room dealing with her children.

B. Lynn tells her she isn't willing to spend the night alone in a motel room bristling with witching wires, so Wumpo has a choice: she can sleep with her mother in her mother's bed, or she can sleep with her mother in her own bed—either way, her mother calls dibs on the side closest to the bathroom. Wumpo's brain writes everything on her face so B. Lynn can tell she is trying to decide if she has a witching wire problem or a mother problem.

Stalking to the nearest witching wire, Wumpo stands on her tip-toes and gives it a tentative sniff, because she is a sniffer. She's sniffs everything. She sniffs around like an ill-mannered mutt—and B. Lynn has told her so—but she always defends her dog-ish behavior saying, *I don't sniff CROTCHES, MOM.*

B. Lynn yells, "Don't breathe in the smoldering evilness for chrissakes," causing Wumpo's head to startle-spasm. It is then they discover a nose serves as a fine tool for removing witching wires from motel woodwork: unable to isolate itself from the spasmodic head, her nose shudder-bumps the witching wire out of the woodwork and into the air.

It soars and twirls before landing on the floor, teetering obscenely between their feet. B. Lynn shrieks, "Jesus CHRIST!"

Wumpo shrieks, *Dammit to HELL!*

B. Lynn shrieks, "You watch your mouth young lady."

They gaze silently at the loathsome thing, and then Wumpo nudges it with her toe. The nudging provokes the wire to twitch which provokes them to repeat the shrieking sequence. They study it for a few more minutes. Wumpo finally says, *Pick it up.*

B. Lynn would give her life for her daughters—and they know that—but she draws the line at certain things and picking up a witching wire is one of them. She says, "You pick it up."

Looking at B. Lynn through eyes clouded with thirty-nine years of hostility and mother issues, Wumpo leans over and tweasers it between her thumb and forefinger. Holding it straight out in front of her body like a one-armed zombie clutching a large upholstery needle, she shoulders through the door and walks carefully across the parking lot to her room.

A few minutes later, Wumpo slams into B. Lynn's room. Holding the witching wire in B. Lynn's face, her hand trembling with her love of her mother, she says, *They're used-up incense sticks, MOM—and Medium A wants to know what the heck are witching wires.*

B. Lynn looks at her, nonplussed—and if you have never been nonplussed—it's a damned uncomfortable feeling.

***

B. Lynn's sister is always warning her about bedbugs. B. Lynn doesn't believe Soozie-Bells has ever been personally involved with any; she thinks she claims experience with bedbugs to make her life sound more dangerous and exciting.

B. Lynn doesn't have much interest in bedbugs, and tells her so. But Soozie-Bells says the first time she stays in a motel rustling with bedbug infestation, she's going to regret her cavalier attitude because they have been known to pack their suitcases and follow people home. They will multiply and establish squatter's rights in her house.

Despite B. Lynn's lack of regard for the subject, her sister has successfully planted a little cocoon of bedbug dread in a dark corner of her brain and it begins unraveling whenever she stays in a motel.

Soozie-Bells has never offered any information about the logistics of bedbug transportation, so B. Lynn has been left to devise her own theories. She suspects they will ride in her hair, lunching on her scalp and playing hide-and seek in her follicles. When she gets home they will search the house for her bed. When they find it, they will hop off her head and immediately begin having sex in her blankets. Their resulting offspring will leave to seek other beds, until every bed in her house is rocking with bedbug copulation.

As she is rinsing Cheese Doodle sludge out of her mouth, so it will be fresh and happy for pizza, B. Lynn notices the sink is littered with whiskers. She feels her gorge rising. Although she doesn't mind being around unfortunate folks plagued with hirsuteness, she loathes hair that is disconnected from a body; renegade hairs are as offensive as runaway scabs or boogers. She believes anything that begins life on a body should stay firmly attached to the body.

Gulping vigorously to counter the rising of her gorge, B. Lynn stares hard and close at the whiskers so she will become desensitized. She has been told this is often a successful method to overcome disconnected hair phobias. Her gorge is suddenly sitting on the back of her tongue because the whiskers have sprouted little legs and they are skittering about like the magnetic shavings in those 'Hairy Harry' games. Her sister's bedbug tales sneak up behind her and throttle her neck. In a haze of terror, she turns and moves swimmingly toward the bed.

B. Lynn's sister is always warning her about the blankets and bedspreads in motel rooms. She says if you shine a special light on the bed it will cause all manner of people residue to blossom on the bedspread. B. Lynn doesn't believe Soozie-

Bells has ever owned a special light; she thinks she claims to know about blossoming residues to ruin her vacations.

Soozie-Bells recommends the demanding of fresh blankets and bedspread whenever staying in a motel, but B. Lynn will be damned if she'll demand fresh blankets and bedspread. If her chamber maid is of a bilious disposition she is likely to rub her face smell all over the linens before bringing them to her. B. Lynn believes people's face smells should stay firmly attached to their own faces. She is surprised the ACLU hasn't taken issue with smells that waft around of their own accord, bothering people who want nothing to do with them. It is inconsiderate and violates people's personal nose spaces. It is flagrant fragrance bullying.

Sucking air into her lungs and holding it secure in case there is a whiff of something worse than face, she employs her fingernails as pincers to fling aside the bedspread. There they are: multitudes of bedbugs dancing on the pillows and frolicking in the sheets. A low moan escapes her mouth, and with the release of air from her lungs the bedbugs vanish. She realizes the holding-in of her breath had been causing explosions of pre-stroke spot in front of her eyes.

She returns to the sink and peers into the basin. Upon careful examination, B. Lynn determines the legged whiskers are nothing more than common sink bugs.

***

It isn't stuffy in B. Lynn's room and the lamps work fine, but the air is dead and so is the light. Posterior-edged against the side of the bed, a method of sitting that doesn't commit her rear-end to an intimate relationship with the unwholesome bedspread, she squints around trying to figure out why the room feels odd.

After several minutes of squinting and figuring she concludes the malignant atmosphere must be a byproduct of death. Someone has died in her room. Because it is a motel room it likely wasn't a friendly death, but rather the kind that requires two people: one person who will become dead and a second person to facilitate the death of the person who will become dead. She has the startling thought that the dull air and light might signify that the room is holding its breath, waiting to see if she will also become dead.

Reluctant to stay alone in a place that is smoldering with despair, she skitters out of her room and across the parking lot to her children's room. She smacks her hand on their door. Discovering the steel door provides an enchanting acoustical effect, she is encouraged to slap-out the drum solo in The Iron Butterfly's song 'In-A-Gadda-Da-Vida.' As her family is confined in the room behind the door, it is a good opportunity for them to appreciate her mastery of the intricate rhythms. Grooving, she adds her own composition of fancy hand work before ending with a final solid smack.

Suctioning her ear against the door, she listens for her children's cries of astonishment at her musical prowess. But other than the thwappings of insects, intoxicated with the shine of the light above her head, there is only silence. After several moments, Wumpo's voice rips through the quiet: *WHAT.*

B. Lynn spooks her voice into megaphone hands pressed in the crack of the door and says, "Loan shark."

Wumpo yells, *For chrissakes, MOM—WHAT.*

B. Lynn says, "Candygram." The door is flung open with such abrupt violence her feet fast-pedal for balance before she topples into Medium A, who is not holding his arms out in a welcoming embrace. He silently disengages himself from B. Lynn, looks at her with a lack of optimism and then slumps back to his chair and looks at the floor.

Wumpo and the J-Man are shin-bouncing on one of the beds, making them appear as a couple of frogs in a popcorn popper. Since Wumpo had passed the entire day with her legs locked straight so her feet could sunbathe on the dashboard, B. Lynn is surprised they haven't splintered at the knees like old kindling sticks.

Springing into the air, Wumpo says, *What.*

"I'm not sleeping in that room by myself," B. Lynn says. "There's something odd about the place." Medium A snakes a glance at her, indicating he thinks she is the only thing odd about the place.

Crashing onto the bed, Wumpo says, *I'm not going over there to sleep with you.*

"Then I want a kid."

Take 'em all, Wumpo replies.

The J-Man says, *No thank you*—boing—*Bobba, I'm busy*—boing—*right now.* Wumpo yells, *Pie and Geigers go sleep with your grandmother.* Pie and Geigers, hunched on the floor in front the television, slowly rotate their heads and gaze at B. Lynn, eyeballs as blank as Furbies with dead batteries. She is pretty sure she saw Pie shudder before the television yanked her eyes back to the screen.

B. Lynn is perfectly aware her grandchildren find her physically disgusting because she found her own grandmothers physically disgusting. As a result, she takes great care to conceal anything that might be categorized as such. When speaking to her grandchildren she always holds her hand in front of her mouth, so to shield them from spit-mist that might escape her flaccid lips. She is vigilant in the plucking of nose hairs and whiskers; she flosses the crumbling remains of her teeth and checks for nose bad breath. She clothes her feet.

Believing that despite her scrupulous attention to personal hygiene, her grandchildren will not sleep with her because they still find her physically disgusting, causes her to feel a great deal of unfriendliness toward them. She decides Pie and Geigers resemble two little clots of fungi sprouting from the carpet and the J-Man actually looks more like a toad than a sweet little frog.

***

It is a hot and lonely night. B. Lynn scuffs across the parking lot and back into her room. Death air heavy on her head, she resumes posterior-edging against the side of the bed. Her eyes come to rest on the small vinyl cooler that accompanies her on all trips; it holds her healthy food options—although her healthy food options have yet to master the trick of osmosis to get their vitamins and nutrients inside her body.

There is a paring knife inside that cooler and it might come in handy if someone wants her to become dead. Shoving off the edge of the bed she scrambles her hands in the cooler, casting aside a single-serving can of V8 Juice and solitary apple, until she locates the unlucky knife that has never known the pleasure of entering fresh fruit flesh.

She carefully places the knife on the night stand and looks at it for a while. The longer she looks the smaller it becomes. The paring knife is not making her feel soothed. She would feel soothed if she had something more substantial to kill someone who might want her to become dead.

As she is wondering if she can prise the shower curtain rod off the bathroom wall, and considering the usefulness of the Gideon Bible as an instrument for head clonking—although handling the Bible might be more anxious-making than handling someone who wants her to become dead—there comes a tap-tap-tapping upon her door. She eagerly rushes to the door and listens intently for someone to be amusing—

maybe Wumpo! She hears some shifting around sounds. Although she isn't sure a person who might want her to become dead would have the good manners to knock before entering, she scuttles to the night stand for the knife and yells, "What."

Bobba it's me Geigers I want to sleep with you. Weak with warmth and affection for the grandchild who isn't bothered by her physical disgustingness, she throws open the door and leans over to smoosh his dear little cheeks. But Geigers, wily in the ways of grandmothers, deftly skirts around her. He sniffs out the location of the TV remote control, throws himself onto the floor and employs the remote as a machine gun to blast through the channels. B. Lynn realizes she is being used for her television.

After watching several shows, all featuring snotty children who are effectively teaching her grandson how to be hateful, she says, "Time to turn off the TV."

Why.

"Because I said so."

Why.

"Geigers turn off the television right now."

No. he says. Geigers's *No* spears into her ears and then squats on her brain like a stink bug with attitude. She tries to shred that *No* into small pieces, so that she might spit-ball them back at Geigers, but she discovers it is a brick wall word; it is a word with a note of finality about it.

She could try jousting with *No* by saying "Yes" but she suspects her "Yes" would be countered with his *No*. If he had said, say, *Ten more minutes,* there would be room for some verbal maneuvering. She could have then returned with an "Okay," cut him off after five minutes, and they both would have felt they had gotten their own way. She decides it is her responsibility as a grandmother to let the child watch television all night.

To distance herself from sheets that might have a bad reputation, B. Lynn wraps herself in her bathrobe and puts on socks. She spreads a pair of her underpants on the pillow to protect her head.

Lying on her back, watching TV glare dance on the ceiling, B. Lynn is stunned with a sudden thought. She is traveling with the same people who abandoned her at Aunt Larlene's house.

Splash

Froggy, B. Lynn's younger daughter, twists sideways in her chaise lounge, snakes out her arm and pinches her mother's left nostril.

Stunned at the sudden and unprovoked mistreatment of her nose, B. Lynn swears and scrubs at her face with the palms of her hands. "What the hell!" she says. "How many times do I have to tell you to keep your hands to yourself? You're thirty-two years old, for crying out loud."

Froggy thrusts an obscene black nose hair, tweasered between her fingernails, in front of B. Lynn's eyes. She raises her eyebrows and lifts her chin. It is her arch look; she is looking archly at her mother. Froggy has perfected this expression—as well as swiveling her head on her neck, cobra-like, and waving her index finger in the air like a rap singer with a cautionary message.

These are the defensive actions of a very short person. She believes they give the impression she is large and frightening—a person to be reckoned with—and she is right: nobody messes with Froggy when she's arching and swiveling.

B. Lynn slaps her hand away from her face and mops at her streaming eyes with a motel swimming pool towel. "Damn that hurt."

I was doing you a favor, Mother. My sister wouldn't have bothered herself with it—my sister could care less about how you go around in public.

"I don't know why you have to drag your sister into everything—she isn't even here and don't talk to me about favors—I gave birth to you. Stop looking at me like that."

Next time I'll just leave you alone, then. But I don't think other people should have to look at your nose whiskers. It's disgusting.

B. Lynn agrees short black hairs sprouting from inappropriate places on people's bodies are unpleasant things to behold—and they also suggest a lack of intelligence in people who are sporting them. But because she is old, she knows nobody is going to look closely enough at her to notice anything going on with her nose. Her nose could hop right off the front of her face to go hang-out with her ears and nobody would pay the least bit of attention.

Nevertheless, she is compelled to express appreciation for Froggy's solitary hair depilation because Froggy will dog her and shred the subject to pieces for the rest of the day if she doesn't. She glances at her and thinks of an ill-tempered Chihuahua. "Well" B. Lynn says. "Thank you. But next time you might give me a little warning before you go diving into my nose."

Froggy replies, *Yep* and jiggles her foot. B. Lynn sighs and gazes at her grandchildren, Miss Bean and Frank, flop around in a swimming pool that is more utilitarian than inviting.

"I can't believe you're letting those children swim in motel swimming pool water."

I know, Froggy replies. Frank thrashes and churns in the water. Miss Bean is swimming gracefully because she is a nice girl.

Shifting in her chaise lounge—one that isn't deserving of a fancy French name as it is nothing more than a precarious aluminum frame held together with occasional strips of frayed nylon—it occurs to B. Lynn that her rear-end might be squeezing through the gaps of the nylon strips so that it might look as if her torso is perched on a harvest moon with smaller planets hovering beneath it. She cautiously reaches under her chair to explore for fleshy protrusions.

Froggy leans forward and slides her eyes at her mother. *What are you doing.*

"I'm trying to feel if my rear-end is squishing through the holes in my chair."

Froggy is quiet for a moment and then says, *What about mine—is mine?* B. Lynn ducks her head to peer under Froggy's seat.

"Not yet," she says. Froggy's foot grows more agitated and she becomes involved in biting the skin on her lips. B. Lynn tells her someday she's going to chew her face right off her head; Froggy abruptly leaves off lip nibbling in favor of picking at her cuticles. These pastimes require all her concentration and are often accompanied with the mindless humming of Christmas carols. She will be useless as a companion until she is happy with herself.

Tired of her daughter, B. Lynn's attention wanders to the people plopped on the other side of the pool. Her eyes skim away from a man and woman—they are old so she doesn't want to look at them too closely—and land on a puffy adolescent girl slumped beside them. She looks depressed and B. Lynn wonders if that's because she's with two people she doesn't want to look at too closely or because she is a puffy adolescent girl.

She jerks her head toward Miss Bean to see if she is showing signs of impending puffiness. Although she is only eight-years-old, it is never too soon to be vigilant about the unwholesome aspects of puberty.

Frank is ingesting large quantities of pool water. He is a notorious vomiter, he throws-up all over the place and he's been doing it his entire six years. B. Lynn tells Froggy, "Your son is going to throw-up."

Froggy says, *No he isn't.* She stands up and yells, *Frank you get out of that pool if you're going to throw-up. I mean it.* Frank nods, chokes, sinks and bobs. His mouth explodes like a can of root beer that's been left in a hot car.

Froggy leaps from her chair and yells, *What did I just tell you!*

B. Lynn says to Froggy, "What did I just tell you." Miss Bean shrieks and the old people across the pool quietly pick up their towels and shuffle out the gate, the depressed and puffy adolescent girl plodding behind them. The product of Frank's eruption drifts like a noxious algae across the surface of the water.

Miss Bean scrambles out of the water and collapses onto the cement apron of the pool, sobbing about the horror of it all. *It almost touched me,* she says.

Frank hauls himself up the pool ladder muttering a mantra, *I'm okay—I'm okay— I'm okay.*

Froggy and B. Lynn silently contemplate the defiled water. Froggy says, *How long do you suppose it will it take the filter to suck up his disturbance?*

"I don't know. A couple of days? Christ. I don't know."

Well let's get the heck out of here and pretend we don't know anything about it. Froggy nudges Miss Bean with her foot and says, *Get yourself off the ground and get over it— we're leaving. Frank wipe-off your face.*

"We can't do that," B. Lynn says. "What if someone brings their innocent little baby out here and they don't notice right away that they're letting their innocent little baby splash around in some other kid's throw-up. How nice is that? Besides, those old people probably just went in to tell on us."

She looks up and scans the motel windows to see if anyone else witnessed her grandson's miserable behavior. Her eyes stumble on her husband, Art, waving and grinning from their third-story room. He is excited B. Lynn can see him all the way up on the third floor.

Art has an aversion to scenes and situations so B. Lynn knows he probably isn't aware of Frank's desecration of the pool—otherwise, he would be acting as if he doesn't know them. He has spent the better part of their thirty years of marriage acting as if he doesn't know B. Lynn.

She turns to Miss Bean and Frank and says, "Wave to your grandfather." Miss Bean lifts a limp hand in the direction of the motel.

Frank screams, *I'm okay!* Art waves and grins.

So, Froggy says. *What should we do.* B. Lynn tells her what she should do is go tell the Front Desk Lady and be quick about it that's what she should do.

You go, says Froggy.

B. Lynn doesn't believe it's her job to go. "Why should I have to go?"

Because I have to take care of my children.

Observing Miss Bean, a hapless puddle of granddaughter quivering by the side of the pool, and Frank looking as though he might be thinking about another good reason to throw-up, B. Lynn decides she would prefer to have to go.

Resting her chin on the counter in the motel lobby, B. Lynn thinks about calling her congressman. The height of this counter is yet another example of the blatant discrimination against very short people. In order to appear as more than a nose and a couple of eyeballs, it is necessary for her to wobble on the tips of her toes and employ her chin as a stabilizer. She might clutch the edge of the counter with her fingers to assist her chin, but too often she has been identified as Kilroy, and she would just as soon people didn't think she was a relic from WWII. She has the right to stand at counters like a normal person and it's time someone in Washington knew about the situation.

The Front Desk Lady is absorbed in herself and so she is not immediately aware that there is a head perched on her counter. B. Lynn says, "Hey." The Front Desk Lady snaps her head in B. Lynn's direction and is surprised to see someone has left her a jack-o-lantern.

She calls across the lobby to a curmudgeonly-looking fellow, hunched in a chair and glaring at a newspaper, *Is it Halloween already?*

Frowning, he replies, *It's July.*

Well why would somebody leave me this pumpkin—I didn't know they even made pumpkins this time of the year.

There's a very short body attached to that head.

The Front Desk Lady stretches across the counter to get a look at the very short body. Satisfied that, indeed, B. Lynn is not a Halloween decoration, she says, *Yes?*

B. Lynn whispers, "My grandson just threw-up in the swimming pool." Because she is conversing with the handicap of limited jaw movement, what with her chin resting on the counter bearing the full weight of her head, the front desk lady grapples for an understanding of the information she has just received.

What?

"My grandson. He threw-up in the pool."

What, repeats the Front Desk Lady, not wanting to grapple with the information she has just received and now understands.

B. Lynn edges back from the counter so that her jaws can move freely and yells, "MY GRANDSON JUST THREW-UP IN THE SWIMMING POOL."

The fellow sitting in the lobby hisses; it is a hiss tinged with disgust and B. Lynn wonders if having a grandson who throws-up in motel swimming pools categorizes her as white trash. She is glad Froggy thought to manicure her nose.

"We don't know how long it will take the filter to suck-up his disturbance."

The Front Desk Lady thinks for a moment and says, *I don't know. Probably a couple days. I don't know.*

"Well. Could you tell the Pool Boy?"

I am the Pool Boy.

"I thought you were the Front Desk Lady."

The Pool Boy replies, *I am the Front Desk Lady.* She slams a plastic sign onto the counter, informing folks she will return shortly, and stalks out of the office.

Trailing behind her, B. Lynn observes she possesses great length of slender body and leg, encased in a black pencil skirt that travels to the tops of her knees: B. Lynn adds this injustice to the list for her congressman. The Pool Boy is openly taunting and flaunting a body and legs that will accept a pencil skirt in a pleasing manner—an obvious case of micro-aggression targeted at very short people. If B. Lynn wanted to experience wearing a pencil skirt in a pleasing manner, the effect would be that of a black plastic lawn and leaf bag bulging with junk: if she can't look precious in a pencil skirt than nobody should.

In addition, she is wearing shoes that artificially increase her height, of which she already has plenty. Anyone over five feet tall should be prohibited by law from wearing shoes that give them an even greater excuse to look down upon people. B. Lynn hopes her congressman is low-statured.

Shoving through the gate to the pool area, the Pool Boy strides an abbreviated pencil-skirt-stride past Froggy, idly toying with a scab on her knee and humming Joy to the World, and pauses to pat Miss Bean on the head. *You're a nice girl,* she says. She stops sharply in front Frank and then sidles around him to fetch a net from the little Pool Boy house.

Miss Bean shocks her eyes at the net and cries, *Nobody told us there's fish in there, too.* She yanks her towel over her head and moans. The Pool Boy swats at a tic in her eye and taps her left foot—displaying considerable athletic prowess by her ankle, as it must elevate her toe from the lofty position of her heel. She gazes glumly at Frank's disturbance that has rearranged itself into a multitude of colorful lily pads drifting serenely upon the water.

Clattering to the edge of the pool the Pool Boy, hampered by the strict confines of her pencil skirt, bends stiffly from her waist and reaches out with the fishing net to prod gingerly at a nearby lily pad. Her maneuvering serves only to terrify the thing: it quickly skates away and clings to a lily pad friend for safety. Frank yells, *You almost caught him!—I want a turn.*

The Pool Boy has little use for Frank and believes he is a distasteful child; she ignores him and angles toward another lily pad, teetering dangerously on her shoe-heel spindles. It occurs to B. Lynn the potential exists that she will tip over into the water and she should make a decision that will serve her better in preparation for the event: send ESP messages to the Pool Boy encouraging her to take a swim with the lily pads in retribution for her bigotry against very short people—or take care of the business herself in case she needs her to clean-up something else later on. Also, the Pool Boy might be the Clean Towel Lady and the Continental Breakfast Server in which case B. Lynn would like to be her friend.

"Here—let me do it." she says.

You're not allowed.

"What do you mean I'm not allowed."

Only Pool Boys are allowed to mess around with the pool.

"Who says."

The Rule People.

This information excites B. Lynn and makes her all the more determined to be the lily pad boss: if there is a rule available for breaking she wants to claim the satisfaction of doing so. And the lily pads came out of her grandson which makes them almost like family—and nobody is going to tell her what she can and can't do with her own family.

She snatches the fishing net away from the Pool Boy and makes a wide sweep at the lily pads, so alarming them they give birth to twins and triplets. The Pool Boy is looking at her with an expression that indicates what she thinks about very short people who think they can be Pool Boys, and so clearing the water of Frank's disturbance becomes a matter of honor and a defense of her limited stature in the world.

Holding the fishing net aloft, B. Lynn wades down the steps of the swimming pool and moves cautiously into the water, taking care to not over-stimulate the lily pads. Miss Bean shrieks and Frank swallows a lumpy swallow. He whispers, *I'm okay.*

B. Lynn says, "Frank look at me. I want you to remember this. I want you to look at me and remember how much your grandmother loves you to get in here with your disturbance so you can go swimming again."

Miss Bean says, *I'm not getting back in there with the fish.*

Me neither, says Frank.

Concert Tour

B. Lynn gazes out the car window and sighs. Wumpo recognizes the tone of her mother's sigh because she quite often uses it herself. *Are you going to pout now?* she asks. "I'm just very disappointed. I never ask you to do anything for me—not a single thing. I hope you think about this when I'm dead—that you wouldn't take the time to drive me back to the motel so I could get my short red coat."

Wumpo jerks her eyes away from the road to look at her mother, *What do you mean 'when you're dead'—are you sick?*

"I'm sick that I raised a daughter who won't do anything for me."

Swear on my life you're not sick.

"As far as I know I'm perfectly healthy—but odds are I'm going to be perfectly dead any minute now if you keep looking at me instead of the road. I don't know why you and your sister think people want you to look at them while you're driving—people actually appreciate a driver who looks at the road every once in a while.

You didn't swear on my life. Mom. If you're sick you need to tell me. Wumpo squeezes the steering wheel until her knuckles look like chicken drumstick ankles, picked clean and sucked dry, and her lips suffer a mild epileptic event. She has little faith in her mother's ability to not die or tell the truth.

"I am not going to swear on your life. What if I'm sick and I just don't know it yet. What happens then—what happens if I swear on your life I'm not sick and it turns out I am? Where does that leave you?" Wumpo glumly stares at the road and mulls over the risk of her own well-being if her mother is sick and doesn't know it.

"I don't know how I'm supposed to enjoy seeing Paul McCartney without my short red coat," B. Lynn says. Wumpo sighs and B. Lynn recognizes the sigh because she quite often uses it herself.

Mother you don't need your coat.

"Look at me! I'm wearing my nice red boots and this scarf here with some red stripes in it and now it's going to look like I don't know how to put together a decent ensemble—my short red coat was supposed to tie everything together so my boots and scarf make sense. Stop looking at me."

Nobody cares about what you're wearing.

"Well I care. I wanted to look nice. That's all." B. Lynn plucks at her scarf and grunts over her seat belt to look at her boots squatting dumbly at the ends of her legs.

I forgot my jacket—you don't hear me carrying on about it.

"That's because yours is just some old generic thing anyone could wear—it's a going to the grocery store kind of jacket. You could wear it to take out the trash and nobody would think a thing of it."

Wumpo considers this for a moment. *What about the rest of me—does the rest of me look like I'm going to the grocery store?*

"Well. I'm not sure anybody cares about what you're wearing."

***

There are certain Particular Types of Women that unsettle B. Lynn's general laissez-faire attitude about people. They compel her to examine the cleanliness of her soul; they plague her when she is lying in bed at night ruminating about who she would like to be in her next life—providing she gets to choose her fresh persona without any interference from God. She knows if He has any say in the matter, He will likely cram her into the body of a Particular Type so when she returns to earth He can teach her a few lessons about intolerance, humility and kindness.

These Particular Types nest in an alien realm of football games and Country and Western music and, although she knows little else about them, B. Lynn's disdain of their preferences in games and music is enough to make her condemn the entire species. Also, she doesn't like the way they dress.

Standing in a line of people that snakes haphazardly behind them and rambles mindlessly ahead of them, B. Lynn latches onto Wumpo's wrist and tips her head at a frivolous Particular Type of Woman prancing in place directly in front of her. It is a surprising locale to have a sighting of one, and B. Lynn wonders if she realizes she's waiting for a Paul McCartney concert and not a drag race competition.

Curling her left index finger, she points at the Particular Type's jacket with her knuckle—an intentional half-point that can't be construed as a full-point, which would call into question her knowledge of good manners.

Wumpo understands what her mother is thinking because she quite often thinks the same things herself. This similarity in cogitating creates a great deal of anxiety and fatigue in Wumpo's life, as she is waged in a constant internal struggle to prevent these thoughts from dribbling out of her mouth while she's at work or with her friends. She would like to impress upon people that she is a nice person, which she generally is when she isn't thinking like her mother.

In order to distance herself from B. Lynn's filthy soul, Wumpo unclamps her wrist and hisses, *At least her jacket looks new and clean—and I'll bet she didn't buy hers at the Good-Will Store —speaking of which, you should thank me for not taking you back to get your short red coat because the hem*

*is unraveling and it hangs down behind you like a flappy tail.
Ha!—or a red diaper.*

The Particular Type reaches up and scatters her fingers around in her nest of cotton candy hair, an alarming yellow that B. Lynn figures was invented specifically for her Type. She then huddles herself more deeply into her nylon jacket, a brilliant beacon of blue that B. Lynn figures was invented specifically for football team jackets.

Wumpo folds her arms and begins torso-twisting, a method of keeping warm that allows her to deny she is cold because she forgot her jacket—rather, she is making good use of her time by engaging in a few aerobics. Perhaps feeling the icy rush of Wumpo's whooshing on the strip of exposed skin pinched between her jacket and skinny black jeans, the Particular Type suddenly swivels around and rakes her eyes up and down Wumpo. *Sweetie, aren't you freezing out here without a coat?* she asks.

Wumpo jolts to a stop in mid-twist, positioning herself in such a way that her face is turned away from her mother. She replies that no, she is not the least bit cold—in fact she is comfortably warm. The Particular Type tilts her head and nods. *Hot flashes, huh? Christ I've been there and done that—and I'm real glad to be finished with the whole nasty business. Believe me—the hot flashes are worth it.*

B. Lynn can't imagine her ravaged post-menopausal face thinks it was worth it, too—and then it occurs to her that they have endured a mutually tragic physical and psychological experience. She reappraises the Particular Type with a modicum of empathy, a sniggling of sisterhood. She sends a tap on the shoulder up to God so he will take notice of her generous feelings.

Rooting her fingertips around in the pocket of her jeans, the Particular Type digs out a depressed pack of Juicy Fruit gum.

She pops a stick into her mouth and extends one toward B. Lynn. It is a sagging stick, wilted from the squeezing warmth of its captivity and B. Lynn is reluctant to take it. She doesn't like the proximity of the pocket to another part of the jeans. But the lure of Juicy Fruit is stronger than her squeamishness about the provenance of the gum; she accepts it and scrapes off the sticky foil with her thumb nail. The Particular Type holds one out for Wumpo, but Wumpo has remained paralyzed mid-torso-twist and refuses to acknowledge her.

B. Lynn and the Particular Type face each other, delightedly chomping—and it is cozy, this chewing together; they are gum bonding. B. Lynn decides if this Particular Type knows enough to like Paul McCartney and Juicy Fruit gum she might have some other civilized qualities. She sends up a knock on the head to God so he will pay attention to what's taking place. After a few minutes the Particular Type spits out her gum and says, *I hate it when the flavor gets all sucked out. Giddyup.* She pirouettes and resumes prancing in place.

Wumpo slowly becomes unglued. She turns, leans her head on her mother's shoulder and whispers, *My God, Mom. Do I look that old?* B. Lynn pulls back to get a better look at her and sees a face that hasn't changed in her eyes for forty years.

"Of course you don't. Look at that woman. She's ridiculous."

I hate her.

"As you should." B. Lynn pats Wumpo on the head and figures God is probably picking out her football team jacket at this very moment. Wumpo snuffles a bit and B. Lynn says, "That woman couldn't possibly have a single intelligent thought in her head. I'll bet she watches daytime TV—what do you want to bet she watches the Jerry Springer Show." B. Lynn stares dully at the back of the Particular Type. She is fairly

211

certain she just sacrificed God's good grace in favor of her daughter.

***

They appear as two slabs of raw bread dough—kneaded, molded, and then plumped solidly down for rising on either side of B. Lynn's head. Although there isn't any knobbiness—or even a few hairs that would give evidence they are receiving life support from a leg, B. Lynn is fairly certain they are, in actuality, a set of very white knees—and they belong to a hefty fellow who has just heaved himself into the stadium seat on the next level directly behind her. The combination of her low stature and the elevation of the seating arrangements cause the knees to rest at the level of her ears so that she feels as though she is sitting in her own little bread dough tunnel.

So she can get a look at her mother, Wumpo leans forward in her seat until her face extends beyond the wall of the left loaf of knee. She hisses, *Mom don't turn around.*

B. Lynn is not likely to turn around—or make any sudden movements, for that matter. Startling the knees could give rise to a knee-jerk reaction resulting in her head being firmly clamped between them—and having her ears sandwiched as such, she might not be able to hear Paul McCartney sing.

So as not to cause the knees any undo anxiety, she holds her head immobile and keeps her eyes locked in a forward position. Concerned that even the slightest flapping of her lips could provoke them, she asks steadily from behind her teeth, "Why shouldn't I turn around."

You don't want to know.

B. Lynn digests the matter of not turning around until turning around becomes the one thing she would most like to do in her life. "Yes I do want to know."

All I'm saying is if you get in the mood to turn around—don't do it. Trust me. B. Lynn is not inclined to trust Wumpo—anymore than she is inclined to trust Wumpo's younger sister, Froggy. With the advent of husbands and children to protect them, they have taken to abusing her with all manner of trickery.

Mulling over the various ways in which her daughters have plagued her in public, B. Lynn sighs and says "Did you stick a baby carrot in my hair?"

Of course I did. There are all kinds of places to get baby carrots around here. They were selling them at the popcorn stand so I bought us a bunch—mashed potatoes, too.

"You might have brought one from home."

You know my children don't allow vegetables in the house.

Because Wumpo and Froggy quite often secretly employ her shoulders to display various foodstuffs and knickknacks that will ensure strangers take notice and believe she is a deranged and ridiculous old woman, B. Lynn develops an urgent need to examine them.

She instructs her eyes to walk sideways and a blur of white knee dough is just beginning to seep into sight when her left eye digs in its heels and announces it is too worn-out to take one more step. This elicits a response from her right eye—asserting the left eye has no business complaining about being tired when it has farther to walk—did anyone ever think about that?—also, it does not appreciate being dragged along every time the right eye wants to go somewhere—it had been perfectly content right where it was.

B. Lynn tells them it will be fun to experiment with their peripheral vision but that only sets them to shrieking about the possibility of having to look at her brains for the rest of their lives. She tugs them back to center, feeling decidedly side-eyed.

"Did you put a tampon mouse on my shoulder?" she asks Wumpo.

Nope.

"Don't lie to me—that's why you wouldn't take me back to the motel to get my short red coat—you thought it would be a highly amusing spectacle for your mother to watch Paul McCartney with a tampon mouse perched on her shoulder. Get it off me—and if you've already taken pictures you can just delete them right this minute."

Wumpo digs a sharp look into her mother and then hastily begins to pat and fumble around with herself in case her mother has secreted a tampon mouse on her. *For your information I didn't bring any tampon mice. But you must have or you wouldn't be so worried about them—where the heck is it.*

"I don't believe that's a question I can answer," B. Lynn says. "But I will tell you I have one in my purse for emergency retaliation purposes. Ha! So you better think twice about any funny business."

Show it to me. I want proof it's still in your purse. B. Lynn rummages in her purse and slowly pulls out an un-tubed tampon blemished with ballpoint ink eyes and a happy mouth. Holding it up by its tail, she stretches her arm out beyond the left loaf of knee and wiggles it at Wumpo. Wumpo grunts and then flings herself back in her seat, disappearing from view.

B. Lynn is calculating the ways she might scrunch down on the floor to tie the tampon mouse onto Wumpo's sneaker laces without attracting her attention, when she remembers she isn't supposed to turn around. Cautiously leaning forward, she says to Wumpo, "I'm going to turn around."

Go ahead, Wumpo replies. *But I'm telling you right now that I will not switch seats with you.*

B. Lynn executes a swift and smooth turn-around. Just inches from her face she is confronted with a sprawling portly portion of man anatomy wadded into a pair of madras shorts that are grimacing with the effort of containing the immensity of him.

The uppermost portion of the man looks down at B. Lynn and scratches his overflowing belly, revealing where all his knee hairs have gone into hiding. B. Lynn gives him a dirty look and rotates her head back to the straight-ahead position. "Wumpo!!" she yells. Wumpo's face appears at the edge of her vision. "Will you please ask that man to sit up straight in his seat?"

You ask him. I don't want to.

"I can't very well talk to his crotch for chrissakes—and pay attention to this because right now is one more good example of something you're going to be sorry about when I'm dead. I hope you remember it—I hope you remember the time you made your mother talk to a crotch."

Why do you keep saying that are you—the right loaf of knee loaf suddenly springs into the air, grazes the top of B. Lynn's head, and settles its ankle on top of the left knee loaf. Attached to the ankle is a sockless foot squatting in a slouching sneaker, and it is dangling delightfully close to Wumpo's right cheek.

As Wumpo is preparing to react to this malignant invasion of her personal space, Paul McCartney silently appears on stage, swaddled in an aura of white light. Knowing this is probably as close as she'll get to any kind of god, B. Lynn crosses herself and quickly recites, 'Now I Lay Me Down to Sleep.' She smacks her hand down on top of Wumpo's head and uses it for balance as her feet scramble to find purchase on her seat.

Wumpo shoves her mother's leg and yells, *Mom the guy behind you can't see.*

"Good—he needs to stand up and get some exercise." Wumpo thinks about this a moment and then slaps the foot away from her face. Grabbing onto B. Lynn's hand she pulls herself up.

Tilting, they lean into each other. Swaying, they laugh. Wobbling, they cry when Paul McCartney sings 'Hey, Jude' because that's what they always do when Paul McCartney sings 'Hey, Jude.'

Snapshots in Black and White

Sucking her upper lip and humming a tune more like a sigh, she maneuvered her way down the tiny hall of her 1950s trailer meant for camping but used for living. She resembled her home: round and squat, her hair gray as the silver paint that had faded and dulled from the relentless heat of long Arkansas summers.

She squeezed past the cooking area, too small to call a kitchen, and entered the living area, too small to call a living room. Shuffling on swollen feet packed in dispirited bedroom slippers, she turned and backed up the few inches to the sofa, flailing her hand in empty air behind her as if her fingertips had radar to detect the correct spot for her landing. When she heaved herself down onto the cushions they gasped in surprise at the weight of her.

She puffed her cheeks, blew out a long breath ending in a wheeze, and then thrust her hand inside the top of her house dress. After an impatient bit of humming and rummaging, she yanked out a handkerchief damp from its nesting place between her ponderous breasts that lolled and joined the girth of her stomach. She mopped at her humid face and fanned herself with the listless hankie and she said to B. Lynn: *Mercy, it is mighty warm out today.*

She was very old.

***

He had the physique and gait of a penguin, tipping and teetering as he walked on abbreviated legs that abruptly disappeared into his paunch. Suspenders stretched over his stomach and hoisted his pants, the clasps pulling and puckering the waist band, threatening to tear loose and cause the suspenders to snap into the air like rubber bands with vengeance on their minds.

Thin red lines traversed the immense landscape of his nose, testimony to hard living and hard drinking. Vague rumors circled around him like hints of smoke: whispers of beatings and orneriness, hot temper and the Klan.

Huffing down the hallway, just wide enough to let him pass, he balanced himself with the palms of his hands patting softly on either side of the walls, sheet-paneled walls with aspirations of quality.

He arrived at the sofa, his daily destination in his trailer home of few destinations. Grunting over his belly, he placed both hands on the armrest for use as a fulcrum and then executed a pirouette with surprising grace. He twirled down and springs whined from the bowels of the sofa. Lacking a lap, he lifted his arm for nestling against his chest. He looked down and he said to B. Lynn: *What's up, Kid.*

He was very old.

***

She was solid; heavy but well contained in a navy blue dress. Shouting worn-out family stories, she sprayed spittle and rapped her knotted knuckles on the tablecloth to emphasize her words. She shouted because she was deaf, and there wasn't a single person sitting at her dinner table who was likely to tell her she was hard of hearing, or that they had listened to the same tales six Sundays in a row. She commanded respect, but little affection.

Rising to fetch dessert—she wouldn't be helped—she placed her gnarled hands on either side of her dinner plate and pushed herself into a standing position; the table groaned, but she didn't hear it.

She stumped toward the kitchen on large straight legs packed like meat sausages in fleshy pink support stockings, her feet heavy in black orthopedic shoes. The color of her stockings stretching over skin mottled blue with bulging veins, caused her legs to be a curious shade of lavender. If her crippled hands, legs, or feet pained her, she never admitted to it.

As she was about to enter the kitchen she turned and she said to B. Lynn: *SIT UP AND FINISH YOUR VEGETABLES.*

She was very old.

***

A three piece suit, pinstriped; a white shirt and a neck tie. A gold chain looped from the button hole on his vest disappeared into a small pocket that hugged his watch. A cardigan sweater was his only concession to casual attire: he was innately modest with a strong sense of decorum.

His clothing might give the impression that he was fussy—inflexible. They might suggest he was flaunting his success of owning a home and an automobile, that he kept his family well-fed and well-dressed during a time when other men stood in lines at soup kitchens. But he was a quiet man and kindly, it was never his thought to put himself on display. He was a gentleman who merely dressed with self-respect and dignity.

Imagine this man: slender and erect; glorious hair white as summer clouds. Imagine this man in his three-piece suit, sitting on the floor with his legs folded, 'Old Maid' cards fanned in his hands. Imagine this man.

He gently tucked a dollar bill into the top of B. Lynn's sock, and then held up his cards to cover his mouth and nose. He peered over the images of Fanny Flint and Greasy Grimes; Lotta Noise and Petunia Pill and he said to B. Lynn: *Tee-hee-hee.*

He was very old.

***

B. Lynn's grandparents were very old. She is alternately amused and depressed that her grandchildren think the same of her.

CPSIA information can be obtained
at www.ICGtesting.com
Printed in the USA
FFOW02n1827280518
46842461-49032FF